THE LOVE BETWEEN
MAN AND WOMAN

*"Only a man who is capable of loving a woman,
and only a woman who is capable of loving a man,
is in a position to love friends, God, and humanity
in a genuine way."*

These words in praise of sexual love provide a key
to the thought of Ignace Lepp—priest, psychiatrist,
and one of France's most provocative thinkers. *The
Psychology of Loving* offers no pious platitudes, no
abstract moralizing. Instead, through analysis of
factual case histories, it illuminates human love at
its worst and best, in the counterfeits of incest,
homosexuality, nymphomania, and in the splendors
of happy marriage and intimacy with God.

"Ignace Lepp is the rare example of a priest who
writes intelligently on love and marriage. . . . Every
form of love and affective temperament is focused
on in this unique volume; interesting, frank, lively,
and very enlightening."

—Robert Francoeur, *Commonweal*

THE PSYCHOLOGY
OF LOVING

---

by IGNACE LEPP

Translated by
BERNARD B. GILLIGAN

A MENTOR-OMEGA BOOK
Published by The New American Library
of Canada Limited

To Christel,
and to Ginette and Yves Pedrolo,
whose friendship I treasure

CONTENTS

INTRODUCTION   11

CHAPTER ONE   PSYCHOPHYSICAL SYMBIOSIS

1. The Two Halves of the Whole Human Being   23
2. Is Love Nothing but Instinct in Disguise?   26
3. Love, a "Communion of Spirit"   28
4. The Complex Reality of Love   31
5. First Love   34
6. Blind Eros   39
7. Reciprocity in Love   41
8. Masculine and Feminine Ways of Love   44

CHAPTER TWO   THE CHOICE OF A PARTNER

1. Ways of Approach   49
2. In Search of the Ego's Ideal   52
3. Choices Based on Complexes   56

CHAPTER THREE   PLATONIC LOVE

1. The Loves of Children and Adolescents   63
2. Good and Bad Faith in Platonic Love   68
3. Platonic Love in Neurotics   70

CHAPTER FOUR   LOVE AND INCEST

1. The Oedipus Complex   76
2. Harmful Effects of the Oedipus Fixation   81
3. A Myth Invented by Freud   84
4. Incestuous Love between Brothers and Sisters 87

CHAPTER FIVE   THE "PARAPHILIAE"

1. Narcissism   92
2. Homosexuality   96
3. Lesbianism   100
4. Sado-Masochistic Loves   106

CHAPTER SIX   FRUSTRATED LOVE

1. Emotional Cripples   112
2. The Fear of Love   117
3. The Illusion of Being in Love   120
4. The Unhappiness of Love   125

CHAPTER SEVEN   LOVE AND AGGRESSION   132

CHAPTER EIGHT   MARRIAGE, THE ENEMY
                OF LOVE?

1. The Separation of Marriage and Love
   in the Past   139
2. The Present State of Confusion   142
3. Marriage and Children   147
4. In-Laws   152
5. The Autonomy of the Individual Person   155
6. Seeing the Whole Picture   157
7. Marriage and Eroticism   160

8. Love and the Right of Divorce   163

9. The Cult of Free Love   164

10. In Spite of Everything . . .   167

Chapter Nine   CHAIN-LOVE

1. Don Juan   171

2. Messalina   179

Chapter Ten   THE DEATH OF LOVE   185

Chapter Eleven   THE LOVE OF FRIENDSHIP

1. Metamorphoses of the *Libido*   194

2. The Furtherance of Existence
   through Friendship   196

3. The Bases of Friendship   199

4. Comparison between Friendship and Love   200

5. Each One Can Have Several Friends   202

6. Jealous Friendships   204

7. Friendship between Men and Women   207

Chapter Twelve   THE SUBLIMATION OF LOVE

1. The Process of Sublimation   211

2. The Erotic Symbolism of Mystical Love   214

3. Love Sublime   219

INDEX   221

INTRODUCTION

Problems of affectivity are infinitely more complicated than any of the questions related to the rational organization of human life. Philosophers and moralists have a mission to clarify man's destiny and establish the laws relevant to its realization. But for a long time now, they have consciously ignored these problems. If we leaf through philosophy textbooks, through the manuals of moral theology used in seminaries and by the theological faculties of both Protestant and Catholic institutions, or through the pages of ethics texts employed in schools of education, we can easily see that man is still being discussed as if he were, in essence, a "rational animal." Yet when we think of Hiroshima, of the death camps of Hitler and Stalin, of juvenile gangsterism, and many other characteristic features of our modern civilization, we are forced to admit that our famous "morality according to the dictates of pure reason" has been a lamentable, catastrophic failure.

Neither philosophers nor moralists are ignorant of the fact that the domain of reason does not by any means extend into every realm of human existence. Love and hate, sympathy and antipathy, enthusiasm and discouragement—as well as some of our most unshakable convictions and beliefs—can hardly be said to be ruled by reason. They are obedient to laws that have nothing whatever to do with rationality. Professional philosophers and moralists, however, believe that they must—and can—disdain what appears to them to be "infra-human," and therefore not deserving of recognition in their ideal conception of man.

The lives of saints and heroes are particularly instructive in this connection. Biographers and hagiographers are afraid that they may be dishonoring their heroes if they concede that not every one of their actions proceeded on the basis of mature, rational principle. Many of his admirers would consider it blasphemy, for example, if

11

anyone should acknowledge the fact that a man like Lyautey permitted himself to be guided more often by his instincts and his completely irrational sympathies and antipathies than by an exclusive concern for "the highest interests of France." To many pious persons it would seem sacrilegious if anyone were to suggest that when Jeanne de Chantal stepped over the body of her son in order to carry out the instructions given her by Francis de Sales, she was acting more like a woman who was passionately in love rather than like someone who was operating on the basis of "mature reflection."

The extent to which rationalist prejudice dominates our culture can be estimated when we realize that a great many Christian theologians make an effort to prove that religious faith itself is a "rational act," in spite of the fact that nobody ever arrived at faith as the result of a conclusion drawn from a process of reasoning.[1]

Forgetful that the God of Love is Spirit, Christian moralists have been in the habit of considering affectivity as an attribute of the body, just as much as atheist philosophers. And by virtue of a strange Manichaeanism of a sort—more unconsciously than consciously, of course—they have treated matter in general, and the human body in particular, with infinite disdain. That a writer as intelligent as Simone de Beauvoir can hold Christianity, the religion of God-become-man, responsible for the ill repute to which the body and sexual love have fallen, is something which ought to serve as an excellent subject of meditation for our pious authors.

Many individuals allow themselves to be deceived by appearances and conclude that it is not at all true that the body and love are held in ill repute in our day. As a matter of fact, they believe that if anything, they are being overestimated. The prevalent worship of movie stars, the cult of sports, and the popularity of shows which feature the strip-tease might lead one to believe

[1] Translator's Note: The author does not intend to deny that "evidences of credibility" and an intelligent assent of the mind play an essential role in the total act of faith made possible by grace. His point is merely that the reasoning process does not necessarily come first, *not* that the act of faith is irrational. His point of view throughout this work is that of the psychologist, not that of the moralist or theologian. His judgments and opinions, therefore, have to be understood in a psychological rather than in a moral or religious sense.

that a real idolatry of the body dominates the scene today. Our young "cheaters,"[2] who seem incapable of denying their senses even the smallest pleasure, certainly do not create the impression of being acquainted with the temptation of a disembodied mysticism. Appearances, however, are deceptive. Anyone who is familiar with the well-founded discoveries of depth psychology will have no difficulty at all in recognizing that these very excesses of the cult of the body are an unsatisfactory over-compensation for the lack of esteem in which the body is held in the depths of the psyche. Any form of idolatry is closer to atheism than it is to the true faith.

But moralists are not completely unaware of how important the role of affectivity is—in the form of the passion of love—to the decision of a man and a woman to unite themselves to each other in order to establish that fundamental cell of human society which is called the family. They have a tendency to see in it, however, nothing more than a useful ruse of Providence or of Nature. Whether their object is to people heaven with saints or to insure a great number of future soldiers for the state, in either case, our moralists concede the necessity for an emotional attraction so long as human beings remain incapable of conducting themselves strictly according to the laws of pure reason. They only tolerate love. It remains their ideal for men and women to come together only after mature reflection, and because they have reached the conclusion that together they possess the necessary qualifications for giving birth to healthy children, for providing them with an adequate education, and for building a "real family" for them to live in.

In speaking about the love of God for men and about the love of human beings for one another, there are preachers who construct a baroque conception of "reasonable love" for themselves. If it is a question of the passion of love—which is the only kind of love that is really love—they become frightened because of the tempests it can stir up and the destruction it can bring about on occasion. The earliest Christian thinkers, who were still quite close to the preaching of the apostles, had no hesitation in adopting the philosophy of Plato—a philos-

---

[2] The expression "cheaters" (*tricheurs*), is borrowed from the title of Marcel Carné's film.

ophy in which the role of Eros is predominant. Such a philosophy seemed to them to be "baptizable." It was not by chance, and not primarily for intellectual reasons, that the theologians of the Middle Ages caused it to be supplanted by the rationalism of Aristotle—a rationalism which contained the seeds of modern positivism and materialism. The theologians in question belonged to an order which had been established for the purpose of combating the Albigensian heresy in Languedoc. Albigensianism owed a great deal to Manichaean dualism. As so often happens, those who set out to combat it came under its influence and contracted its disdain and fear of love. The beatific vision itself had now to be conceived in terms of an "intellectual act," and not in terms of an affective communion.

We have alluded to the serious practical consequences wrought in our civilization by the misunderstanding and downgrading of love. In the realm of speculative philosophy, it has ended up in an absolute idealism which goes so far as to doubt—or even to deny—the existence of an extra-mental universe, and which could not help but provoke its own antithesis, atheistic materialism. In the domain of ethics, a pragmatism inspired by Kant on the one hand, and a casuistry which incorrectly calls itself Christian on the other, have succeeded in depriving the minds of a great number of individuals of a true sense of morality. When we consider how long this intense battle of Reason against Love has been going on, it is actually astonishing that its effects have not been more devastating. In spite of everything, it is still possible to find real goodness in the hearts of men. It is still possible to observe generosity at work in their actions. This is no small reason tending to support an optimistic view of human nature. It witnesses strongly to the fact that love is really a constitutive factor in our psyche.

To paraphrase and adapt the saying of Pascal, we might observe that for many centuries now man has had pretensions to being an angel, and has entertained the desire to become a "pure intelligence." The catastrophe that has befallen him, however, is worse than what has been predicted for him by the great seventeenth-century moralist. It is not a beast that man has become, but a robot. And, certainly, that is hardly better.

I do not wish to disparage the efforts being made by social reformers. Quite the contrary. I am convinced that they are engaged in a noble and useful task, but a terribly thankless one. I myself was one of their number for years, persuaded that I was working for the happiness of mankind. By degrees, however, my experience and personal reflection brought me to come to the realization that the world never would become better and men happier until human beings learned to open their hearts, and to put greater warmth and love into their relationships. The betterment of the material conditions of life and the marvellous progress of science and technology will not be truly "good" for man unless they are placed at the service of men who know how and are willing to love.

The kind of love that the reader will find extolled in the pages of this book, as we investigate the conditions for its ideal realization, will not be an abstract, "purely spiritual," disembodied love. What the world requires and every human being urgently needs is love that is truly human. Such love is both physical and psychological at the same time. Only a man who is capable of loving a woman, and only a woman who is capable of loving a man, is in a position to love friends, God, and humanity in a genuine way. This may seem to be insisting on the obvious. It is true that everybody everywhere talks about love. But the individuals who really know how to love are actually very rare. They are much rarer even than those who really know how to think.

The various Christian churches, and all those who are concerned with the happiness of individual men and the future of mankind, do not fully appreciate the great services that can be rendered their cause by the different forms of depth psychology. They fail to appreciate the positive contributions which depth psychology has already made.[3] I do not enjoy playing the role of prophet, but I would not be at all surprised if future historians attribute to the revolution inaugurated in psychology by Freud an importance equal to the Copernican revolution

[3] Translator's Note: Nevertheless, a beginning has been made, as can be seen in the work of John C. Ford, S.J. and George G. Hagmeier, C.S.P.

in astronomy, Pasteur's revolution in microbiology, and Einstein's revolution in physics.

Not that everything contained in Freud's theories of affectivity is pure gold. It is inevitable that those who are engaged in combat against overly rigid systems of thought and inveterate prejudices will not fail to avoid constructing new systems of their own which will be just as rigid as the older ones, exaggerating to absurdity the opposition between the old and the new. This is what happened in Freud's case, and it happened to an even greater extent in the case of those who consider themselves his most faithful disciples. The reader will observe that whenever there is a reference to the theses and hypotheses of psychoanalysis in this book, they generally are treated with many reservations. Freud can be excused on the ground that he is a true son of the ultra-rationalism and scientism of the nineteenth century. However violent his own reaction against it, he could not help being influenced by it. It left its imprint on him. The same circumstance cannot serve as a valid excuse, however, in the case of his disciples.

It was the unquestionable merit of Freud to have undertaken to restore affectivity, and especially love, to the primary role it actually has to play in human life. Other depth psychologists, who came after him and were largely inspired by him, have since probed the obscure and hidden recesses of the psyche to such an extent that it is no longer presumptuous today to speak of a true science of the soul.[4] Love is no longer the special preserve of the poets and novelists. It has become an object of scientific knowledge. The patient labors of C. G. Jung and his school have contributed to this knowledge in a very special way.

Let us forget about theories for a moment and take a look at the way in which men actually behave. Is it not immediately apparent that love—more so than reason— guides them, motivates their actions, and gives meaning and significance to their lives? When we declare that a

[4] This is a fact that is far from being recognized by everyone. It still frequently happens that on radio programs and in the newspapers one can find psychoanalysis placed in the same category with astrology, occultism and other "esoteric sciences." This is a manifestation of gross ignorance, since psychoanalysis can take its rightful place alongside biology and medicine.

man is happy—and all the more so when we declare that a woman is happy—we are seldom referring to the degree of perfection they have attained in the acquisition of rational truth. We usually do not intend to draw attention to the fact that they are rich or that they enjoy an enviable position. To declare that someone is happy is to signify that he is, or that we suppose him to be, enjoying the height of emotional fulfillment. All the evidence points to the fact that it is not by chance that love constitutes the main theme in all folklore, literature, the plastic arts and the advanced religions of mankind.

Since everybody talks about love and everyone actually experiences love to some extent, it might be thought that no notion could be clearer and more precise than the notion of love. The truth, however, is just the opposite. Like every other profoundly existential reality, love can barely be defined. Is it not the most commonly used verbs—to be, to have, etc.—which are also the most irregular in their conjugation in any language? What does the still half-animal instinct urging two "primitive" individuals to come together have in common with the all-consuming, but never assuaged, passion of Prouhèze and Rodrigo in Paul Claudel's *The Satin Slpiper?* How can there possibly be any similarity between the sentiments which inspire the characters in the novels of a Françoise Sagan and the love for God displayed by a Saint Teresa of Avila?

In a work written some years ago,[5] I attempted to disengage the "essence" of love from an accumulation of definitions and descriptions of it furnished by philosophers and poets. The majority of the conclusions I arrived at then still seem valid to me today. In the present work, however, I do not propose to develop a philosophy of love, but rather a psychology of love. It follows, therefore, that I shall have to resort to a fundamentally different method of procedure. In the present work, my own experience in depth psychology will serve as the point of departure for my inquiries and reflections.

The Psychology of Loving is an ambiguous title. Only human beings, after all, and not their emotions, are capable of being analyzed in a psychological fashion. If

[5] *La Communication des existences,* Editions de la Colombe, 1951.

custom still sanctioned the lengthy, complete titles authors of former times were addicted to, this book would have to be called, *Reflections on What Depth Psychology Teaches Us About Love*. It is true that love itself—or any other emotion—cannot be the direct object of psychological analysis. Every individual who is analyzed, however, is involved in one way or another with love. What he has to teach us about love is worth infinitely more than any theoretical speculation about the subject.

Psychology of love? Psychoanalysis of love? More precisely, I would say, *psychosynthesis* of love. My debt to Freudian psychoanalysis—and still more to the analytic psychology of C. G. Jung—is very great. In my daily practice as a psychologist, I never cease to benefit from their teachings and their extensive observations. For a long time now, however, I have been convinced that analysis alone is completely inadequate. By itself alone, it cannot further the psychological balance and the happiness of human beings. This conviction was also held by Jung and a number of other depth psychologists. Neuroses and psychological conflicts too greatly undermine the personality of an individual to enable him to succeed all by himself in the task of constructing a new synthesis of his existence once he is liberated from the complexes that have been inhibiting him. In addition to analysis, the psychologist's task is to help the subject to find an affective reality of a positive character to take the place that was formerly occupied by his neurosis. If psychoanalysis does not lead in any way to a psychosynthesis, there is a danger that it may do more harm than good and so tend to justify the suspicions against it which many persons still entertain.

I shall not be content with just analyzing the various forms of normal and abnormal love. There is nothing in this book that will teach the specialist anything new. My aim in this book is a more modest one. It is to help people to love, to help them to love in a better way, and to show them how to face up to the suffering that comes from the absence of love. I would hope, in a work of synthesis of this kind, to be able to contribute modestly to the furtherance of love in the life of the individual and in the collective life of all mankind.

The affective energy known as the *libido* is not restricted to serving the purpose of sexuality between man and woman on the physical level. Filial love, paternal love, maternal love, the love of art and the love of philosophy, the love of God, all these are not called love in only an improper and metaphorical sense of the word. If this were a philosophical treatise, "erotic love" (that is, love between a man and a woman which tends in the direction of sexual gratification) would make its appearance as only one among many different possible incarnations of the idea of love. There would be nothing in such a conception that would not be in conformity with the truth. From the standpoint of the psychological method of analysis and synthesis adopted in this book, however, it becomes necessary to assign first place to the love that exists between two persons of the opposite sex. It is this type of love, as a matter of fact, which more than any other leaves its imprint on human life. This is true even when it is prepared for and conditioned by other types of love. It is also a fact that it is in connection with this type of love that the majority of problems and difficulties arise. It is here that the most tragic of the deviations of the *libido* can occur. After we have observed and analyzed the many different aspects of erotic love, we shall be in a position to understand more clearly other types of love. Essential similarities, however, must not be permitted to obscure differences, and vice versa. It is absolutely correct to state that *eros* is not all there is to love; it remains to be seen, however, whether it is not true that *eros* is present as an ingredient in every form of love. If *eros* is established as present in every form of love, it remains to be considered then whether we have the right to declare that all forms of love are but different variations of erotic love.

There are many different forms of abnormal love. Homosexuality, sadism and masochism, impotency and frigidity are so many different types of emotional illness. Their unfortunate effects on the individual and on society are at least as great as those produced by cancer or by polio. Can such sicknesses be prevented? Can they be cured? Or is it perhaps necessary to resign ourselves to their presence?

To these and many other questions, a psychosynthesis of love must try to find satisfactory answers. Note that I have written, *"try to find* satisfactory answers." I do not pretend to have discovered all the answers. The science of psychology is still too young for anyone to be astonished at the fact that it is not able to provide any more certitudes than even much older sciences are able to furnish in their respective domains. In the case of so vital a matter as love, it would still be very valuable if we succeeded in doing nothing more than shedding some light on the subject.

It has already been pointed out that the contents of this book are not addressed to specialists, particularly not to specialists in psychoanalysis. It is true that the majority of our preoccupations will coincide with theirs. It is not our purpose here, however, to defend any particular school of thought, but to attempt to afford an opportunity to educated people to benefit from an acquaintance with the all but absolutely certain insights and conclusions of depth psychology. At the same time, it is not the aim of this book to offer the reader a "popularized version" of anything, in the pejorative sense in which this phrase is used by the "experts" who lecture and write for the general public. It is not the intention here to adapt theories developed by technicians for the benefit of other technicians to the supposedly low level of the general public. This book is the direct product of my own long experience in depth psychology. I naturally have confronted my own experience with that of the masters of depth psychology and of several of my colleagues and friends. My aim is above all a practical one. I have deliberately avoided presenting an "esoteric" exposition of the subject as much as possible, because it would be comprehensible only to professional psychologists.

The reader will find very little theoretical discussion in the pages of this book. As far as possible, an attempt has been made to present the different aspects of the enormous problem of love in terms of concrete examples. The reader will be in a position, therefore, to make comparisons with his own experience and observation.

The majority of the "cases" cited as examples are taken from my own personal experience in normal and abnormal psychology. A few of them have been made available to me by psychologists whose extensive experience and moral and intellectual integrity I respect. I have also borrowed certain examples from the works of some of the most famous masters of depth psychology, especially from C. G. Jung, Charles Baudouin and W. Stekel.

It would be useless to try to recognize "actual individuals" behind the "cases" discussed in this book. I have deliberately "constructed" each of the cases, paying attention to observations made about real individuals only to the extent that certain elements proved to be indispensable for the reader's comprehension of the essential point. Frequently, I have placed under the heading of one case observations relating to several different individuals. In certain instances, I have left out something which was unique to a single individual.

Many of the situations described in this book are more or less of a nature that is seriously pathological. It is to be hoped that no pessimistic conclusions about love will be drawn from this fact. It is simply that in pathological cases the phenomena one is studying are found in an exaggerated state. They are, consequently, easier to observe in that way than when they are found under their so-called "normal" conditions. A caricature sometimes expresses the truth in a much better way than a photograph.

CHAPTER ONE

PSYCHOPHYSICAL SYMBIOSIS

ACCORDING TO the ancient myth, recounted by Plato and found in several ancient traditions, mankind originally existed in an androgynous form, each individual being at once both male and female. As a punishment for some mysterious crime, however, the gods split man into two. Ever since then, the two halves of this single creature have sought, with varying degrees of success, but never with complete success, to restore their disrupted unity. The agonizing search for this lost androgynous unity is what we call love.

1. *The Two Halves of the Whole Human Being*

There is obviously no point in trying to discover in this myth any trace of historical truth. It is surprising that so intelligent a man as Freud should succumb to such a temptation, not only in the case of Oedipus, but in the case of this myth of an androgynous man as well. It is all the more surprising in view of the fact that Freud professed such absolute faith in the positivist scientism of the nineteenth century.

The fact that one should not try to uncover historical truths in myths does not mean, however, that they have nothing to teach the psychologist. This is especially true in the case of myths that are found, with more or less significantly different shadings, among different peoples living at great distances from one another. The Jungian theory of *archetypes,* the foundations of which are hardly debatable, is a remarkable case in point of psychological truths that have been transmitted through the vehicle of mythology.

The biblical story of Eve's creation out of Adam's rib conveys under a different form the same truth that is in

23

the Platonic myth: Man and woman are indispensable to each other. They need each other and complete each other as two halves of one whole. This is evident on the biological level. The propagation of the species requires the intimate cooperation of both sexes. We have this in common with every other species of sexual animal. But the complementary nature of man and woman is equally unquestionable on the psychological plane as well. It seems to become more accentuated the more the human psyche evolves and becomes ever more complex and differentiated. We shall have occasion to note several times in the course of this study how, if male-female relationships are placed almost exclusively at the service of the species among "primitives" and "rustics," and at the service of society as well among men who have attained a higher development, the relations between highly civilized men and women are infinitely more profound, with the spiritual clearly taking precedence over the biological and the sociological. On the supposition that technical progress with parthenogenesis might one day render superfluous the physical cooperation of both sexes for the propagation of the species, it seems to me that man and woman would hardly become less indispensable to each other on the psychological plane.[1] It is not at all permissible to view them as antagonists, necessarily in competition and at war with each other.

Certain noteworthy differences between masculine and feminine psychology are observable. A man, roughly speaking, is an extrovert. He is active and oriented toward the domination of the external world. As a result, thought and sensation are more highly developed in him than feeling and intuition. A woman, on the contrary, seems more the introvert. She is more passive. Intuition and sentiment predominate in her. This, however, is simply a matter of statistical classification on a broad scale. No account is being taken of individual characteristics which often belie these typical traits. It is no longer forbidden to hold, with Simone de Beauvoir, that if the majority of women are more passive than active, more introverted than extroverted, this is not necessarily be-

[1] Both of them would also be indispensable to the child born by parthenogenesis, whose harmonious development is difficult to realize with the help of the mother alone.

cause of their "nature" but because of their "situation." It is due at least partially to the fact that the evolution of human society has relegated them to a type of existence which hardly calls for the practice of "the active virtues." In any case, absolutely nothing authorizes us to postulate an unbridgeable psychological abyss between the two sexes.

Metaphysical speculations on the essence of masculinity and femininity are not our present purpose. Remaining strictly on the level of psychological observation, we can state that in practice the majority of women are "feminine" and the majority of men "masculine." The line of demarcation, however, is really less rigid than it is customarily conceived to be.

If men were one hundred per cent masculine and women one hundred per cent feminine, they would constitute—psychologically, at least—two heterogeneous species. They would not be complementary to each other. There would not be any need or possibility of communication between them. The exclusively introverted woman would live in a dream-world. She would be as inapt for action as for reflection. The completely extroverted man, entirely taken up with the external world, would be inhumanly hard, incapable of understanding not only others but himself as well. Lacking intuition, he would be unsuited for any truly creative activity. He would be enslaved to a terrible materialism, and closed to all forms of spiritual life. Between a woman who was "perfectly" feminine and a man who was "perfectly" masculine there could be sexual intercourse, but no love. Sexual intercourse itself, in such a case, would not be a union between two people, but a sado-masochistic combat. A certain limited number of examples of such cases can actually be found.

Fortunately, this is not the normal situation. Jung's theory of *compensation* explains perfectly how man and woman are infinitely more complementary than opposed to each other. In persons who are not too inhibited by a neurosis, their unconscious compensates spontaneously for what is too one-sidedly present in the individual's conscious *ego*. A completely feminine woman who loves a man who is very masculine does so because of the presence of certain so-called virile qualities in her own unconscious psyche. That is why she finds herself able to understand and "sympathize" with him. Specifically feminine traits can be found in the unconscious of even the most masculine of men. No doubt this is the reason a "masculine" man can understand and appreciate a "true woman" better than an effeminate man can. As we shall have occasion to see later, love is authentic in proportion to the degree of the authenticity of the masculinity and femininity of the partners. An effeminate man and a virile woman resemble each other too much to be truly complementary.

2. Is Love Nothing but Instinct in Disguise?

What name should be given to the mysterious force which draws men and women toward each other? Certain sexologists who have had their day think they are manifesting their scientific spirit by being intent on "depoetizing" the complex phenomenon called *love*. They claim that love is nothing more than a more or less acute, temporary or chronic infection of the organism caused by the secretions of the sexual glands. Strictly speaking, a surgical or medical operation on said glands could cause love to be born, to die, and to be modified at will.

Charles, a twenty-four-year-old medical student, stoutly upheld theories in the presence of all his comrades, according to which love is nothing but a biochemical reaction, a sort of magnetic attraction between the ovaries and the glands. With youthful confidence in the authors he had read, our future medico proclaimed that whatever is "poetical" or in the order of sentiment in love is nothing but instinct more or less successfully disguised. Too proud and cowardly to recognize himself for what he is, man wants at all costs to consider himself different from the other mammals. Consequently he has to believe that there is something more than the biological and the chemical in the violent attraction he experiences for his sexual partner. Charles was firmly convinced that the theories he defended were scientifically established on the basis of what psychoanalysis, thanks to experimentation, teaches us about the instincts in general and about the sexual instinct in particular. Wishing to be consistent with his theories in his relations with women, he regularly avoided any "emotional entanglement," anything which seemed to him not strictly necessary for the satisfaction of a need which he believed exclusively physiological in character. As a result, his relationships became inhumanly cold, not only with his sexual partners, but with his parents, brothers and sisters, and friends as well. Refusing friendship as much as love, he saw enemies everywhere. A neurosis of a manic-depressive character, a "persecution-mania," finally led him to the office of a psychiatrist.

Freud is not directly responsible for theories which pretend to reduce love to a biochemical complex of some sort. As in the case of Charles, the responsibility rests particularly with a neurotic aberration. It is incontestable, however, that certain psychoanalysts who call themselves Freudian furnish such a neurotic aberration with a sort of rational justification. Much could be said about the neurogenic activity of the simplifiers of Freudian doctrine. As for Freud himself, the most serious charge one can bring against him is that he has provided them with the example of his own method of reduction, a method which tries to explain the higher in terms of the lower: "This is nothing but that"; "Love is nothing but sexual instinct."

To understand Freud, one must never forget that he was—as much by his intellectual formation as by his own turn of mind—a true offspring of the scientific nineteenth century. At that time only the natural sciences had any right to the name of science. How could he avoid identifying human instinctual impulses with the instincts of the animals? He was too keen and too honest an observer, however, not to discern the fundamental originality of psychological activity; on the level of concrete existence, it is impossible to reduce this to biological reaction. Not considering myself personally a disciple of Freud, it is that much easier for me to concede to Christian Freudians that the founder of psychoanalysis has done more, in practice, to combat a certain kind of pseudo-scientific materialism than many of the most zealous, self-appointed, defenders of "spiritual values."

That much being said, it has to be acknowledged that the greatest confusion nevertheless reigns in the Freudian interpretation of love. The term is taken as a perfect synonym for *libido*, which itself is taken to be *nothing but* sexual instinct. Is it permissible, however, and in what sense, to speak of a human sex instinct? Human sexuality involves so many elements not related to instinct in any way, particularly among normally developed human beings, that a purely biological theory of the instincts is absolutely inadequate to account for them. Thus, for example, studies of sex among animals tend to support the conclusion that no animal experiences sensual pleasure in the act of intercourse, whereas the role of pleasure is of primary importance in the case of human sexual activity. Sensual pleasure goes far beyond the implications of a biological instinct. It is characterized at least as much by factors on the higher psychological levels as by those on the physical level. To avoid ambiguity, therefore, it is preferable in the case of the human being to speak of sexual attraction instead of sexual instinct. In that way it will be possible to convey the idea that, even on the level of the "physical," there is in human sexuality something other than the physical. It is particularly true of love that it is not reducible to simple sexuality, even when it is a question of a "psychologicized" sexuality.

3. Love, a "Communion of Spirit"

Elizabeth, who was thirty years old and married for eight years, said she loved her husband very much. She would have loved him more, however, if only he would have consented to consider their love a purely spiritual communion. The fact that he could desire her sexually, "like animals in rut," profoundly disgusted her and offended her "human dignity." As a result, she could not love him as intensely as she would have liked. On certain days she even detested her spouse.

Having received a very puritanical education (up to the very time of her marriage), Elizabeth practically ignored everything having to do with sex. She thought conception took place as a result of kissing and that birth occurred through the navel. There was still a great confusion in her mind between sexuality and the excretory functions. In confession, she accused herself of having "impure thoughts" when, not wanting to get up at night, she experienced the insistent need to void her bladder. Yet this woman had an excellent high school education!

Elizabeth had read a good deal of poetry as a young girl. The extreme feeling of shame her education had inculcated in her prevented her from understanding the poets' allusions to the realities of love. She constructed for herself an exclusively spiritual—or rather ethereal—idea of it. The most she dared allow herself to imagine was the exchange of tender kisses between a man and wife. It is understandable how traumatic the first night of marriage was bound to be for her, especially since her husband seemed not even to have suspected anything about the illusions and feelings of his young wife.

If she had to, she was willing to admit that "one does that" in order to have children; although she bore a grievance against God for not having invented a "cleaner" way of transmitting life. Things being the way they are, however, she was nevertheless prepared to perform her conjugal duty, asking only that it be done without any desire or passion. But above all, "that" must not be called love.

Needless to say, Elizabeth was completely frigid. Worse yet, she wanted to remain frigid. If occasionally she experienced a furtive pleasure of the senses, she experienced it as a humiliation and accused herself of having made a profanation of love. Since it was not possible for her to love her husband in the way she understood love, that is to say, without the slightest participation of the flesh, she went in for friendly exchanges with men she believed she had no need to fear would want to do "that," particularly priests. When she learned that her husband had a mistress, she felt it was an unpardonable betrayal on his part.

The case of Elizabeth is a good example—although clearly to a neurotic degree—of a certain "angelistic" conception of love which is more widespread in our era than one might think. Its advocates and adversaries both are wrong in attributing this conception to Christianity. On the contrary, this radical opposition between a principle of good—the spirit—and a principle of evil—the body—had been borrowed from oriental dualism by neoplatonic philosophy. In spite of their admiration for Plato, the early Christian writers felt instinctively that such a duality did not in any way conform to the spirit of the Gospel. It was only very much later, under the combined influence of medieval heresies and the puritanism of the Reformation and Jansenism, that Christian teaching permitted itself to be imbued with scorn for the body.

It remains undeniable, however, that for several centuries Christian preaching has contributed greatly to the diffusion of ideas which tend to dissociate love from sexuality. It is scarcely half a century ago that in France the Abbé Violet had the courage to denounce this dangerous error, taught in the very name of Christianity. Fortunately, priests of the younger generation today are rare who believe it necessary to speak with disdain of the body in general or of sexuality in particular. The moral ideas of the Church find their echo even in quarters which consciously desire to remain far removed from her, and where sometimes even the most radical kind of libertinism is professed. It is permissible to hope, therefore, that the reevaluation of sex on the part of Christian moralists will not be slow in having beneficial repercussions beyond the Church's fold.

One cannot expect too rapid a revolution, however. Many mothers of families, many good sisters and other persons whose influence on the formation of the young is great, are not yet prepared to follow the new approach opened up by the moralists. Many of them are scandalized by the instruction in sexual matters imparted to youth by young priests in study groups. Are these groups not partly responsible, they ask, for the fact that youth today seems to attach less importance to the traditional notion of "purity"?

The psychologist too has to understand the unconscious motivation behind this resistance to liberation from sexual taboos. Many religious are frustrated in the matter of love. They have taught themselves to despise what they have been obliged to renounce. To acknowledge the beauty of sex would involve the risk of shattering the fragile edifice of a spiritual sublimation that has not succeeded very well. Many married women have never experienced anything in sexuality but boredom and fatigue. How can they tell their daughters that there is anything beautiful or grand about sex? But an understanding of the resistances that exist does not prevent us from thinking and saying that the pretension to a love that would be purely spiritual, from the Christian point of view, implies a serious religious error and a dangerous threat to psychic equilibrium.

The human being is indissolubly composed of body and soul, matter and spirit. This is so true from the Christian point of view that the renowned Cardinal Saliège has had the courage to declare publicly that it is difficult for him to believe in a real distinction between the two components of the human composite. It would be wrong to be scandalized at this and to cry heresy. Theologians and philosophers who consider the body and the soul separately are looking at them from the standpoint of essences, while the Archbishop of Toulouse sees them in a perspective that is existential. Existentially, there is nothing human that is not simultaneously—although in different degrees—both matter and spirit, both body and soul.

We must also remember that when the psychologist speaks of "the soul," he is not declaring for any metaphysical theory. For him the soul is the equivalent of the psychic totality.

4. *The Complex Reality of Love*

It was pointed out before that in the human being, instinct is never something exclusively biological. Eating, among humans, is not put exclusively at the service of the conservation of the individual. This is not a matter of the excessive refinement of a decadent civilization. Our feasts and banquets actually correspond to one of the basic exigencies of the human "composite." Everyone agrees that a man's life is not really "human" if he is reduced to the position of simply satisfying his strictly biological need for nourishment.

Of all the instincts, the sexual is without doubt the one in which the psychological and the biological are the most interwoven. More than with the instinct for food, it is necessary in the case of sex to take issue with the application to human beings of theories about the instincts of a purely biological nature. It would not even be true to say that sexuality constitutes a side of love that is *physical*.

It is extremely difficult—if not impossible, as a matter of fact—to distinguish the physical from the psychological components in the existential reality of love. In the course of history, as gradually and in proportion to the extent of human evolution love became ever more complex, the role of the psychological became ever more preponderant.

In his interesting work *Les trois échelons de l'érotisme,* Emile Lucka assumes that in the beginning—that is to say, among human beings not yet sufficiently evolved— love was exclusively sexual in its character. Like an animal, the male was attracted to the female solely on the basis of instinct, an instinct put wholly at the service of the species. Later in the Middle Ages, under the influence of a Christianity hostile to the body, love became purely spiritual and metaphysical. Finally, the civilized man of today aspires to a perfect symbiosis of sexuality and spiritual eroticism.

There is a certain amount of truth in this view. Like all schemata, however, it is oversimplified. In particular, the notion of the succession in time of the three modes of love does not conform to history in any way. The courtly love of the Middle Ages, for example, was very much less exclusively spiritual than a superficial reading of certain poems of the troubadours might afford one the opportunity to see. It was rarely addressed to a legitimate spouse, and sex was not at all excluded from its eroticism. It was not until after the Renaissance, under the combined influence of the Reformation, the Counter-reformation and Jansenism, that the ideal of a purely spiritual love became rather general in the West.

In speaking of a spiritual eroticism (which he distinguishes from the purely sexual), Lucka is very much closer to the truth of experience than many psychoanalysts. It is also true that the further the human being is from his primitive state of animality, the more his love becomes spiritual. In the case of certain crude individuals, even in our own civilization, the sexual drive has been modified so little by feelings of tenderness and admiration that it is scarcely any different from what can be observed among the higher animals. I have actually known a number of persons, who belonged to the leisure class and who had received a fair amount of education, whose sexual life seemed devoid of all affectivity and who were not even capable of understanding the meaning of the word "love." If they happened to hear it on the lips of a singer or a preacher, they spontaneously interpreted it in the sexual sense of "making love." It is impossible to consider them as "simple-minded," for in other respects they often showed themselves very intelligent. It infallibly turns out in analysis, however, that such persons have remained children emotionally. They are "perverse," but perverse individuals who could very well have become normal persons except for the psychological inhibitions that either arrested or distorted their emotional development.

The majority of men and women in our civilization are neither simple-minded nor perverse. It is still the physical which occupies first place in their relations with the opposite sex, but the psychological, the "sentimental," is already very much intermingled with it. To possess the heart, one has to approach it by way of the senses; but the senses do not obtain any true satisfaction unless the heart cooperates.

Among those we might call the élite of mankind, in persons whose emotional development has kept pace with their intellectual development, it is with the heart that love normally begins. The senses enter into the picture only secondarily. As we shall have occasion to note when we speak of love between saints, the place occupied by the psychological or the spiritual can become so preponderant that apparently nothing more of the physical remains. It is wise, however, not to trust appearances.

Physical or sexual attraction is seldom absent in human love. At most it is susceptible of spiritualization or sublimation. In any case, it is always dangerous to pretend to exclude senses from the love between a man and a woman unless the partners have attained a very high degree of spiritualization in the totality of their existence. If they have not, they can expose themselves to dangerous illusions.

I knew a sixty-year-old poet who for years cultivated the most sublime spiritual love for one of his feminine admirers twenty years his junior. In their letters and conversations, they were an example to each other, treating "carnal" matters with scorn. That is, until the day the poet arrived unexpectedly at the house of his beloved. She was away, and he tried to violate her fifteen-year-old daughter. There is no reason whatever to accuse this man of hypocrisy. With perfect sincerity he could say that he did not understand what "had come over him." The depth psychologist, acquainted with the mechanism of *identification*, knows very well what "came over" our poet. It was his beloved whom he was attempting to possess in the guise of her daughter.

5. First Love

Theoretically, all human beings are predisposed to love. They find themselves in a latent state of amorous expectation. The universality of this predisposition and expectation inclines us to believe that they are innate, somewhat like the aptitude for speech and free choice. In our own, and other civilizations as well, however, they are buttressed considerably by literature and art, the principal theme of which is everywhere love. In a country like France where, at least in the big cities, the sense of shame has largely disappeared and lovers display their feelings in the subway, the streets and other public places, children do not long remain ignorant about the exact nature of the movements of the heart they find themselves experiencing for a friend of the opposite sex.

At the age of eight, Bernard seemed not to have paid any attention to the couples who used to put their arms around each other's waist and kiss and hug each other in the public park where he played every day. When he was eleven, he began to notice it. He was amused by it, but he never thought to ask himself what such gestures meant. A little later on, he began to have dreams in which he too would hold a young girl by the waist, or be kissing her. The young girl usually "had no face," but sometimes he recognized her to be a young girl a little older than himself who lived nearby. About the same time, love stories began to interest him more than adventure stories. Sometimes his dreams and reading were accompanied by an erection or a nocturnal emission, but he established no connection between the two sets of facts. It was only when he was thirteen years old that Bernard became conscious of being in love.

Not everyone possesses the predisposition to love in the same degree. Individuals are as unequally endowed emotionally as they are intellectually. It frequently happens too that individuals born with a rich affectivity see their amorous predispositions inhibited by various psychological and sociological factors. In order for them to realize their normal capacity for love, they generally have to experience a certain psychological liberation. It is significant that most neurotics are persons whose affectivity has remained at an infantile stage of development or has become distorted in one way or another.

"It is precisely through love, and through love alone," writes the poet, André Breton, "that the fusion of essence and existence is realized in the highest degree." It is particularly the first experience of love that has exceptional existential significance. This is true almost as much in the case of a man as it is in the case of a woman, although generally a woman is more conscious of it. The emotional maturity of the individual depends to a great extent upon the character of this first experience. It very often gives a definitive coloration to later experiences, and professional and social success are largely conditioned by it.

There hardly seems to be any intrinsic connection between the first sexual impulses and the awakening of the emotional life. Quite the contrary. One often observes a radical separation between these two realities. It is especially noticeable with boys, but on closer inspection it can be observed almost as frequently with girls as well.

James was twelve years old and hopelessly in love with his cousin, who was eighteen. He secretly followed her on her walks, and was jealous of her admirers. He buried his face in the clothing she had worn, and dedicated poems to her in which he compared her to the heroines of his favorite novels. He dreamed of her every night, but always in an absolutely "chaste" manner. He saw himself sleeping in the same room with her, but naturally in a separate bed, and he never saw her undressed. James had had the occasion to see men and women kiss each other on the mouth. He experienced the desire to take a young girl into his arms. But that she should be his cousin, or that another man should kiss her, such an idea seemed sacrilegious to him.

Just about that time, James began to experience his first erections, and his sexual impulses became exceptionally intense for one of his age. Nocturnal emissions were frequent, and he masturbated excessively. He deliberately imagined himself in erotic situations with young girls of his own age, but almost always with one toward whom he was antipathetic. One day he even tried to have intercourse with one of them who was mentally defective.

Viewed superficially, the case of James would seem to confirm simultaneously the opinion of those who see in sexual desire nothing but a biochemical reaction, and the opinion of those who see love written necessarily in capitals and as tending "in itself" only to a communion of spirit. The cousin is the one who represents love, and the girls are the ones he wants to possess.

Observing his habit of masturbation and other character difficulties, in desperation James's mother sent him for psychological treatment. During the course of treatment, it soon appeared that it was precisely toward the cousin whom he loved that the boy's sexual desire tended. His *superego*, however, was composed of prohibitions and censures, and was abnormally rigid. Under its domination a split was effected between his love feelings on the one hand and his sexual desires on the other. Since his *superego* forbade him to desire the one whom he loved, his sexual desire transferred itself completely spontaneously to those who resembled as little as possible the object of his adoration. This same psychological process can be observed at work in certain adults also. A man feels himself all the more guilty of adultery if he takes for his mistress a woman who resembles his spouse morally or physically, or if she belongs to the same social class. On the other hand, he feels himself almost "in order," if not with regard to Christian morality at least with regard to what he believes are his obligations with respect to his wife, when his sexual partner for the occasion is a prostitute, a maid, or at least a person as different as possible from his wife.

As well founded as our observations are, however, we should avoid making generalizations. In the case of certain children, there is actually no connection between the first impulse of their sexual instinct and love. It goes without saying that in granting this hypothesis we are speaking of sexual impulses in the strict sense of the term. Naturally, if (with Freud) we were to characterize as sexual the pleasure experienced by the small child in the arms of its mother, it would then evidently be impossible to distinguish between love and the sexual instinct. But it is not to be excluded a priori that in certain cases love can be present without any link to sexuality. One must not let himself be deceived by appearances, however. We have seen how with James sexual desire could be completely repressed in the unconscious. We shall have occasion to make an analysis of "platonic love" later.

First love is rarely lasting. It generally manifests itself at an age too early to take on any definitive commitments. Besides, in the course of his development toward maturity, the individual undergoes much too radical a transformation to be able to remain faithful to his first passion. It does happen, of course, that a man of thirty will marry the young girl who had been the object of his first ardor. Most frequently, however, he had no longer even been thinking of her over the years, and it is with a new and adult emotion that he now directs himself toward her and she toward him. Each of the partners has been in the position of achieving his own maturity, and it has been achieved in such a way as to make communion between them possible.

By contrast, a definitive engagement between two people who are still too young entails the risk of eventual unhappiness. The chances are very strong that they will no longer have anything in common when they both have become adults.

Fleeting as it may be, the first love is almost always of great importance from the psychological standpoint. It never fails to have an influence, for good or for ill, on the loves to come. That is why the psychologist puts so much emphasis on the fact that the first love should be a successful emotional experience. The young boy or girl who first falls in love with a person who is unworthy of love, with someone capable of abusing the confidence placed in him by a pure and inexperienced heart, has diminished his or her chances of ever again being able to love wholeheartedly, with that trust and complete abandon which every authentic love dictates. Failures in love (as well as successes) are almost always produced in a series. But where the layman speaks of "fate," the depth psychologist has no difficulty in recognizing the inner causality involved.

Lisa, fifteen years of age, pretty and sentimental, like many young girls of her age, was hopelessly in love with her literature professor, who was almost three times her age. She wrote him love-letters and dedicated poems to him. More daring than most girls, she saw to it that her idol received them. He was flattered at the thought of being the young girl's flame. He invited Lisa to his home. He embraced and caressed her, and soon made her his mistress. He tired of her very quickly, however, and without much ceremony finally got rid of her.

Unhappy and resentful, Lisa decided to be blasé about it and pretended she no longer believed in love. For several years, she went from man to man (some of them loved her) without experiencing herself as capable of the least emotional attachment to any of them. At twenty-two she married a man who really loved her and whom she respected. But she did not succeed in attaching herself deeply even to him. She often betrayed him. She would have tried to obtain a divorce except that she realized she would not be any the more satisfied with any other man. In the course of a brief psychotherapy (undertaken for a completely different reason), it became clear that Lisa unconsciously identified all men with the unworthy object of her first love whom she had long ago ceased to think about consciously.

To illustrate how a first love can have a positive influence, I shall choose an example from among the numerous cases I have had occasion to observe. This case closely resembles the case of Lisa.

Anne became the mistress of her piano teacher at sixteen. She did not have the feeling that she had been seduced, and the man—who seems to have loved her as much as she loved him—always treated her with great kindness. They separated a year later when Anne had to go to another town to complete her studies. She suffered a great deal because of it, but she never felt she had been betrayed. On the contrary, she was convinced that he was affected at least as much as she. She loved other men after that and eventually married for love. Far from preventing her from cherishing her husband, the experience of her first love seems to have helped her. Thanks to this experience she continued to believe firmly in love. Of course, she had "forgotten" her first love.

6. Blind Eros

The obstacles encountered by love are numerous. As with all difficult things, the first necessary step toward success is one's belief in it. Love involves the symbiosis of such strong psychological currents that every young, healthy human being believes in it spontaneously. If this is not always the case in practice, it is due to inhibitions which have deflected affective energy from its normal path, or to certain traumatic experiences which have blocked it. The case of Lisa exemplifies the situation of a relatively late "traumatization" of faith in love. The spectacle presented by parents who are not in love or who love each other very little is often another unconscious cause of the lack of faith in love sometimes encountered in young people.

Every human being is predisposed to love. He aspires to it and considers love the essential criterion of his success in life. If there are a great number of men and women who, unfortunately, do not achieve love or do not succeed in their efforts to find love, it is because the emotional development of many individuals is arrested at an infantile stage. Men and women of great intellectual achievement are often emotional "cripples."

It is not only a matter of unconscious inhibitions. Affectivity, as much if not more than intelligence, has need of being educated. To say that "love learns by itself how to breathe and walk" is nonsense, unless one considers love a mere whim. Even breathing and walking require training if one wants to do these things correctly. Numerous ailments are due to poor breathing, and everyone knows that an excellent carriage has to be acquired. With all the more reason is a period of training required in the case of a psychological activity as complex as love. In the rationalistic civilization in which we live, the reason so many adults love so poorly (to their own harm, the harm of those close to them, and of humanity in general) is that the importance of teaching the young how to develop their emotional potentialities is so badly understood.

Novelists and poets are not completely wrong when they describe love as being a kind of emotional intoxication. In its intense states it reminds one of drunkenness or of mystical ecstasy. All the other psychological powers find themselves considerably inhibited if not absolutely paralyzed. It is not surprising then that in such a state a lover tends to overestimate the character of the object of his passion. Since the latter is identified in certain respects with his own ego-ideal, he spontaneously projects the whole content of this ideal onto it. Others often find ridiculous the enthusiasm with which a lover speaks about the one he loves. They know the individual in question to be a completely ordinary person.

Mr. F. had made life unbearable for the woman he loved because of his jealousy. Persuaded that of all women she was the most desirable, he assumed that every man she knew and every man he knew was her lover. To cure him of this morbid jealousy, the psychotherapist had to bring him to recognize that the woman he loved was no more beautiful or intelligent than thousands of others just like her.

It should not be concluded too readily on the basis of pathological cases, however, that experimental confirmation has been found for the old saying, "love is blind." In the normal person who is in love, it is only the faculty of objective, rational knowledge that is weakened by passion. This is generally true, moreover, only for a certain period of time, while the subject is wholly absorbed in the conquest of the object of his flame. As soon as he possesses it, he is no longer blind to failings and defects. Love, however, makes it possible for him to accept the limitations of the beloved.

When it comes to subjective, deep, existential knowledge, however, only the lover is capable of it. He alone is in a position to recognize the hidden treasures of the one he loves. He can recognize not only what the beloved is, but also what the beloved has the potentialities to become.

Therese, a pretty night-club singer, about twenty-five, came to me to help her "become a new woman." Several persons who thought they knew her well had already spoken to me about her. Some of them expressed disdain for her frivolousness, her vanity, and the exceptionally loose character of her morals. Others made fun of certain speech defects she had, and of the furtive way she had of looking at a person. But the man who was passionately in love with her also spoke to me about Therese. From him, I never heard anything about her speech or about her furtive glance. Although he was aware that the singer was flirtatious, he was ready to swear that she was nevertheless neither frivolous nor loose. He said she was understanding and affectionate. He attributed the immorality of her life to the fact that she was extremely unhappy.

At first one would obviously be tempted to believe Therese's critics and think that love had blinded the person who sang her praises. Since he had not noticed the physical defects of the woman, would it not be logical to conclude that he also was completely unaware of her moral character? But as I found out for myself, it was he who was right, and not the others. Love had made it possible for him to divine possibilities in Therese which even she was unaware of. In addition to that, it was his love that would give her the strength and courage to come to the realization of her true self.

Genuine love is the most effective creator and promoter of human existence. If many persons who are well (or even moderately) endowed nevertheless remain mediocre, it is often because they have never been loved with a strong and tender love.

7. *Reciprocity in Love*

Theoretically, reciprocity is not at all necessary for love to be "true." "Does it concern you that I love you?" The main thing is to love. The person who loves is already no longer alone, even if the object of his love does not return his sentiments, or even if she completely ignores them. Besides, is it not generally true that when a man notices that he is in love with a certain woman, he seldom conveys his feelings to her? As we shall have occasion to note further on, it is also true that adolescent love has little concern for reciprocity, which in no sense prevents it from being very genuine. There are individuals who love another person passionately for years, or even an entire lifetime, without any requital whatsoever, sometimes without their even daring to look for any. From a psychological viewpoint, such one-sided love is far from being altogether sterile. I have known several persons whom it has helped to bear the burden of a completely humdrum daily existence more cheerfully. In his novel, *Je vivrai l'amour des autres*, Jean Cayrol has demonstrated with a great amount of delicacy and depth the fertile power of solitary love.

Such love is exceptional, however. Normally, love does not fully realize its function as a promoter of existence except through the communion it establishes between two partners, each of whom recognizes the other as his perfect equal.

It is fairly common for a man to possess the body of the woman he loves without any real reciprocity, either because he has bought her or violated her. A woman in love can also have a man for her husband or her lover whom she knows very well does not love her. In both cases, however, sexual union loses precisely what gives it its character of human nobility: the fact that it is the symbol and expression of a communion of souls.

Strictly speaking, the party who is not in love can consider himself or herself satisfied. A man may marry the woman who loves him because of her money or because he counts on her to facilitate his climb up the social ladder. A woman may marry a man who loves her just for the sake of "marrying well" and not remaining an old maid. Or she may be willing to become his mistress out of vanity or self-interest. If these objectives are attained, what have they to complain about, especially when their affective needs find their satisfaction elsewhere?

As for the one who is in love, however, he or she will necessarily become disillusioned with such a hybrid liaison. Even if he or she is not conscious of it in the beginning, it is always something other—something much more—than sexual pleasure that is expected from the person loved.

Mark courted Anne assiduously for years. He loved her passionately, and it was his most ardent desire to make her his wife. She did not hide the fact that she felt only sympathy for him, and only the slightest physical attraction. This seemed to her not enough to hold them together for life. Partly from lassitude, partly from ambition (he belonged to a much higher social class than she), but particularly because she had recently experi-

enced a painful disappointment in love, Anne finally gave
in and married Mark.

Life with a man of refinement, passionately in love
with her, and who assured her of very agreeable material
conditions of life besides, was not lacking in charm in
Anne's eyes. It was true that her heart did not beat for
him at all, but several flirtations afforded her some emotional experiences that were at least partially satisfactory.
She reasoned that since her husband had known before-
hand that her heart was not his, she had no obligation to
deny herself what was offered her in this way. It seemed
to her that her only duty was to be discreet, and not give
anyone occasion to talk about her in any way that would
sully her husband's social reputation or humiliate him.

As for Mark, in the beginning he was very happy to
have the woman he loved by his side. This meant more
to him than that their sexual relations should be satisfying. He congratulated himself for not having retreated
before Anne's lack of enthusiasm. However, when I had
the occasion to meet him seven years after the honeymoon, in spite of all Anne's protestations, Mark had been
firmly hoping that sooner or later she would get around
to loving him all the same. It would take him several
years to abandon all his illusions on this subject. He was
almost prostrate. He lost all liking for work, neglected his
business, and spent the best part of his time observing the
comings and goings of his wife. He became morbidly
jealous, not only with regard to Anne's more or less
serious flirtations, but also of her confessor, her doctor—
even their own son. Naturally gentle and refined, he now
became violent, at times uncouth. He got to the point
where a nervous depression obliged him to seek help. He
finally acquired enough strength to support his life without being loved by the woman he always loved. But he
continued to suffer none the less. Certainly, he never
realized the kind of genuine existence to which he had
aspired in his youth, and to which his gifts and social
position had in a way destined him.

The case of Mark and Anne is not at all unusual.
Knowing he is loved in return gives a person confidence
in himself and stimulates him to make his life a success. It
is true that in many women their passivity is still sufficiently great for them to succeed, frequently enough, in

loving the person who loves them. Their mothers and their various counsellors find it enough that they do not experience any positive repulsion, and accept the advances of the men who love them: "Love will come later." But young women like Anne are becoming more and more numerous, especially in educated circles. Their love is as personal and as active as that of men. It would be dangerous for them and for those who love them to become involved with them unless the love were reciprocated.

8. Masculine and Feminine Ways of Love

There is a very old saying which declares, "A woman does not love in the same way that a man does." The analytic psychologist can only confirm this as a fact. It is astonishing, therefore, that so universal an acknowledgment of this fact in theory saves so comparatively few couples in love from the misunderstandings and sufferings which result precisely from the fact that each of the partners expects the other to love him or her in exactly the same way as he or she loves. "Since he does not love me as I love him," a woman often argues, "it must be because he does not love me as much as I love him." "As" and "as much," however, are far from being synonymous terms.

Byron remarked, "Love is only one occupation in a man's life, but for a woman it is life itself." Balzac, more of an anti-feminist, disdainfully declared, "On the highest level, the life of a man is glory, the life of a woman love," meaning, of course, that there is no glory in love. And Nietzsche, in *The Gay Science,* writes, "The same word, love, actually signifies two different things for a man and a woman. What a woman understands by the term is clear enough. It is not only devotion, but a total gift of body and soul, without reservation, without regard for anything else. It is this absence of a condition which makes of her love a faith, the only one she has. As for a man, if he loves a woman, it is just that kind of love that he *wants* from her. Consequently, he is far from assuming that it is appropriate for himself to have the same kind of sentiment he expects in a woman. If there are men who do experience this desire for total abandonment, it seems to me that they cannot really be men."

These citations, to which we could add many others, are taken from the best literary and philosophical sources. They may seem very peremptory, but they are far from being without foundation in existential reality. It is of little concern to the psychologist whether the great difference between the way a man and the way a woman loves is based on a difference of nature or, as Simone de Beauvoir thinks, on different kinds of education and different modes of life.

Distinctions can legitimately be made between the way the uneducated love and the way the educated love, between the way the Germans and the Italians, scientists and literary people, and so on, love. The problem which concerns us here, however, is one that is much more concrete. As a general rule, the proletariat and the bourgeoisie, Russians and Englishmen, athletes and intellectuals, find love among themselves, within their respective groups. The differences to be found in their ways of loving are of purely intellectual interest to the rest of us. The situation is completely different, however, when it is a question of men and women. This is due to the fact that, as such, they are mutually destined to love each other.

In the life of a woman, love undoubtedly plays the primary role. Sometimes, it is so predominant that the entire life of a woman seems devoted to it. This is true not only in civilizations like Islam, in which she lives within the confines of a harem. Even among us, and to some extent even in the most advanced circles, from the time of puberty on the young girl hopes to make a success of her life and to realize her destiny through love. Her childhood dolls, the books she is advised to read, the conversations of her parents and friends about her future, all conspire to inculcate in her the idea that her principal role on earth is to love and be loved. As a result, all the other duties imposed on her by life appear to be secondary.

In a famous private school in Paris, where boys and girls are educated together, up to a certain age the girls succeed at least as well and sometimes even surpass the boys in their studies. But around the ages of fourteen or fifteen, it is noticeable that if the presence of girls in the class acts as a stimulant to scholarly endeavors on the part of at least the better students among the boys, the majority of the girls—even the ones who were, up until that time, excellent students—give up all competition. It is not that they cease to be "serious-minded." The psychologist who has had the privilege of talking to them knows that it is their budding womanhood that makes them look on the boys no longer as rivals with whom they have to compete, but as representatives of the sex they are "destined" to please and to give themselves to. Only the "would-be boys" among the girls refuse to resign themselves to their "predestination."

Even when a young girl is very talented, has undertaken higher studies, and has prepared herself for some professional activity in which she is interested, it is rare for her to devote herself to it with the same sense of total commitment observable in the majority of men. Women are very rare who are not disposed to abandon their studies or their profession if they deem it necessary for the sake of love. Simone de Beauvoir is undoubtedly right when she considers this psychological predisposition, rather than a presumed innate inferiority, to be the reason so few women produce any great work in their lifetime.

Catherine, a famous lawyer and well-known woman in politics, was past thirty-five when she fell in love for the first time in her life and experienced herself loved in return. The issue of marriage came up. It happened that the profession and social position of the man she loved were incompatible with Catherine's position as a lawyer and with her political activity. There was a prolonged and painful debate. There was a time when her friends would have thought that a woman as active and ambitious as Catherine would not at all mind sacrificing her love to her vocation. However, it was love that carried the day. After fifteen years of marriage, Catherine spoke with nostalgia of her independence and the passionate activities she formerly enjoyed. But with complete sincerity, she insisted that she could not have acted differently, and that if she had it all to do over again, she would do exactly the same thing. It is significant, in this case, that the couple never for an instant raised the question about the man's possibly sacrificing his profession for their mutual love. And this in spite of the fact that from both a material and a "worldly" point of view, his position was very inferior to Catherine's.

It is extremely rare that love occupies so preponderant a place in the life of a man. Here, too, education and social custom probably play as much (if not more) of a role as "nature." A little boy is not given dolls to play with. Instead, he is given models of electric trains and airplanes, a bicycle, or tools. He is not told that when he grows up he will marry, but that he will become a doctor, an engineer, a farmer, etc. While the little girl identifies herself with her mother, who seems completely devoted to the service of her husband and her children, the normal boy identifies himself with his father, who has an occupation and a social function and in whose life a wife and children seem to play another and perhaps a secondary role.

Thus it is that from his earliest years a man understands that in order to measure up, in order to succeed in life, he has to engage in combats which are very different from the combats of love. Under the impact of a momentary violent passion, he can temporarily lose the clear consciousness of this hierarchy, but generally he is not slow in recovering it. What he looks for, more or less consciously in love, is rather "the repose of the warrior," a stimulant for the battle of life, and sometimes justification for the same. This was the situation with Mark, whose case we analyzed before. The failure of his love no doubt caused him to neglect all his other interests too, but this was precisely because he had expected love to be the stimulant he needed for success in his enterprises. Only adolescents and men who are neurotic find themselves in a position of loving the way women do, that is to say, of giving to love (in a permanent fashion) the prime role in their life.

Much unhappiness and suffering could be avoided if both men and women were fully conscious of these differences in their respective ways of loving. It may be that—as our modern feminists hope—one day women will love in the same way as men. They will no longer live for love. Meanwhile, it will be useful and helpful for them to be firmly convinced that if the man they love does not love in the same manner as they, it does not mean he loves any the less. As for men, by keeping in mind the place love holds in the life of their companion, they will avoid causing her to suffer and themselves to experience a painful disappointment.

CHAPTER TWO

THE CHOICE OF A PARTNER

ONE OF the most important and most interesting problems raised by the psychology of love is the problem of how to choose a partner. It is not a question, in this chapter, of a choice with marriage in view. That choice is often motivated by objective factors which have no direct relation to love—factors like chance, the necessities of a career, family situation, and so on. Here we are simply asking ourselves, "Why is it that someone is in love with this one particular person? Why not some other person?"

Obviously, from the objective point of view of a third party, often nothing whatever would seem to justify love's choice. It is not at all unusual for the subject himself to be completely incapable of justifying it. The chosen one, with whom he desires to be united at all costs—sometimes at the price of having to make sacrifices which the day before might have seemed to him enormously disproportionate to the calculated advantages—is not necessarily any more beautiful, more charming, or more intelligent than many another. Frequently just the opposite is the case.

1. Ways of Approach

An individual with little maturity seems to pick his sexual partner almost at random. It is almost impossible to speak of a real choice in such a case. For the man, all that is required is that his partner be a female. There is no need for him to have one particular woman rather than another. For the woman, any male will do. She gives herself—for the time being or forever—to anyone who will have her. I have often asked such men and women why they chose a particular woman or man for their partner, and received no reply. Some of them frankly acknowledged that the individuality of their partner was not a very important consideration for them. It should be noted that "emotional primitives" of this sort are not to be found only among the primitive tribes of Africa or in the lowest rungs of society in our own civilization. They can be encountered even among educated, middle-class people. Emotional maturity does not always go hand in hand with intellectual development.

As a general rule, however, it is true that the more mature an individual is and the more he functions as an independent person, the more complex his choice of a love-partner becomes. The Russian novelists of the nineteenth century even went so far as to maintain that there was only one woman in the world for any individual man, and only one man in the world for any one woman. They were "destined for each other from all eternity." This undoubtedly would limit in the extreme the chances of a happy choice.

Many sexologists and psychoanalysts have tried to explain the motivations behind the choice of a love-partner on a strictly "scientific" basis. Physical qualities, the beauty and strength of the body, certainly enter into the picture for many persons. The eyes, the nose, the mouth, the hair, the legs, the hands, and other parts of the body, are quite capable of consciously or unconsciously arousing in us an attraction for a particular person we may happen to meet by chance. Psychoanalysts tend to see a causal link between the erogenous zone of the subject and the part of the other person's body which exerts the greatest attraction on him. It is not absolutely certain that such a relationship exists. Let us assume, for example, that a certain man is fascinated by a woman's mouth because of the primarily oral character of his own eroticism. This still would not explain why it is that he prefers thin lips to thick lips or thick lips to thin lips. It is understandable how a certain woman can find the look of certain men "irresistible" because she is a "voyeuse" and her own erogenous zone is located in her face. But why, for example, should her sensitivity be restricted to men with gray eyes? There may be some truth in the theory which maintains that a sudden experience of being "smitten by love" is explainable in terms of erogenous zones, but it rests on such a fragile scientific foundation that it would be completely misleading to try to draw any definite conclusions from it.

Certain individuals fall in love not because they are seduced by the beauty of one or another part of another person's body but because they are sensitive to the way the other person's hips move, to the other person's voice, or to the odor emanating from the other person's body. There is a story told about Henry III, when he was Duke of Anjou. During festivities held in honor of the marriage of the King of Navarre and Marguerite de Valois, he went off to a secluded chamber to try to get some rest after a dance. A short time before that Marie de Cleves had changed one of her garments in the same room because it was wet with perspiration. The future king picked up the garment, not knowing to whom it belonged, and used it to wipe the sweat from his brow. Instantly he began to experience a most vehement passion for its owner. When Henri Bergson lectured at the Collège de France many elegant women were overcome with love for the philosopher. There was nothing of the "handsome male" about him, however, and few if any of these women of the world really understood his philosophy. But the voice of the master was enough to fascinate them. When it comes to movements of the body, there are many women who seem to sense its "effectiveness." Often (to their great discomfort) they will wear high-heeled shoes in order to emphasize the movements of their hips.

Physical appeals do not cease to play a role in the case of persons who are emotionally and intellectually more mature. Other factors are added, however, and these often take precedence over physical allure. A musician may be loved for his playing, a painter for his pictures, a philosopher for his ideas, a politician for his success, and so on. A professor of philosophy whom I knew well, a man with a raspy voice, who was short and rather ugly, used to raise real emotional havoc with his female students year after year. Many of them undoubtedly would have paid no attention to another man, regardless of how young, handsome and seductive he might be. But the philosophical ideas of the professor exercised such a fascination over them that, if he gave them the slightest encouragement, they were ready to throw themselves into his arms, propelled as if by some irresistible mechanism. None of them could hope to marry him (they probably would have refused him if he had asked any of them to marry him), and nearly all of them were aware of his well-established reputation as a Don Juan. It should be remarked that the professor's philosophy contained nothing "perverse" in it. It did not exalt sensuality or counsel amorality. In the situations which I was able to observe for myself at close range, the fascination with him was truly of an exclusively intellectual character.

2. In Search of the Ego's Ideal

It is useless—in the majority of cases, at least—to try to explain the birth of love in terms of a single driving force. Generally it is a whole ensemble of causes and a set of extremely complex motivations that serve to ignite the fire of love. Physical and psychological factors are inextricably intertwined, with the predominance of one set of factors at one time and of the other set at another time, even in the same individual. And since unconscious motivations seem to outweigh by far the conscious motives of an individual, the subject himself is almost never in a position to tell us why he loves one particular person. As a rule, it is only in the course of depth analysis that the real explanations for his love are disclosed, and often to the great astonishment of the person concerned.

John stated that he was interested only in brunettes. They were the only type that attracted his attention on the street or in a gathering. By some malicious fate, however, it seemed that each time he fell in love it was always with a blonde. He complained bitterly about it because it seemed absolutely incomprehensible. But analysis disclosed that John's mother was short and a brunette. As a child he had suffered painfully from a lack of affection on the part of his mother, to whom he was very much attached. It was this attachment that explained why his theoretically ideal woman had to resemble his mother. It was his love for her that he wanted to find in short brunettes. But since his adored mother had been a frivolous, worldly sort of person who showed her son very little affection, an unconscious fear prevented him from falling in love with women who resembled her.

Jacqueline had been extremely attached to her father and actually in love with him in her childhood. Later on she frequently had occasion to resent his lack of kindness and his domestic tyranny, to the point where she began to hate him and to revolt against him. Her first amorous enthusiasms were experienced for young men whom she found to be the complete opposites of her father in their refined sensibilities, their kindness and politeness, and even their physical appearance. She never succeeded, however, in becoming deeply attached to any one of them. It was only when she was thirty years old, after she had completed her graduate studies and had achieved an enviable social position, that she met the great love of her life. She did not hesitate for an instant to marry him. It took her several years to realize how great a resemblance the character and temperament of her husband bore to that of her father. Just as her father had been with her mother, Jacqueline's husband was extremely authoritarian with her. He was jealous of his wife's intellectual superiority, as her father had been of her mother's, and by degrees he began to show himself to be just as coarse as her father had been. With age, even the physical resemblance between the two men became accentuated. There is no doubt that Jacqueline's unconscious had never stopped loving and admiring her father. It had recognized the image of her father in the man she fell in love with and decided to marry.

The foregoing examples indicate how the parental image can have very different effects, sometimes serving to account for a repugnance and at other times for an attraction. This fact should preserve us from the temptation to rely upon superficial explanations.

In order to explain all this, there is no need whatever to have recourse to the famous theory of the Oedipus complex, so dear to the heart of Freud and so handy for his followers to employ as an explanation of almost everything. In love, the individual seeks and hopes for his own realization in another person. From the earliest age, an ego-ideal begins to take shape in the psyche of an individual. This ego-ideal never ceases to look for its own realization in all the vicissitudes of life. The construction of this ego-ideal is of the utmost importance for a man's destiny. It serves as a dynamic attraction for him with regard to his development. Innumerable factors, both conscious and unconscious, contribute to its formation. Often enough one or the other of the parents effectively exercises a dominant influence. This is the case every time the psychological maturity of the individual is seen to be inhibited by a faulty education, which has prevented the necessary emancipation from the father or the mother from taking place. When this happens, the choice of a partner in love will undoubtedly be made exclusively in keeping with an unconscious attitude toward the parents.

Frequently enough, the dominant image in the constitution of the ego-ideal is that of a professor, an older friend, an author, an historical figure, or a legendary hero. I knew a lesbian in whose love life the figure of Joan of Arc had played as decisive a role as the mother in the case of John, and as the father in the case of Jacqueline. As we had occasion to see before, the first love often exercises a determining influence on the form taken by succeeding loves. Stendhal has told a story: "There was a certain man who was passionately in love with a very frail, pock-marked woman. Death deprived him of her. Three years later, in Rome, he was admitted to the intimate company of two women. One of them was more radiant than the sun, and the other frail and pock-marked, and consequently rather homely. In a week's time, the man was in love with the homely woman, whose ugliness was erased for him by his memories."

Animals—particularly the female of the species—do not experience sexual hunger except during the period of rut. There is no such thing, strictly speaking, as a period of rut in the case of human beings. Normally, both men and women are capable of experiencing sexual desire at any time of the month or year, provided certain psychological and physical conditions are in tune. At certain particular stages of life, however, love's demands make themselves felt in a rather imperious manner.

In the majority of individuals, the susceptibility for sexual love is particularly great toward the end of the adolescent period. At this time it does not require much to inflame the heart and stir up the feelings. If adolescent love is not very selective, it is probably because the ego-ideal is still fluid, with too many divergent influences operating in the unconscious. It is an observable fact that young people whose ego-ideal becomes fixed at too early an age—especially if it becomes fixed within the context of an Oedipus complex—are practically incapable of falling in love.

There is a second "season" of great susceptibility for love, situated about the height of adult life. This is particularly true in the case of men who have had to fight and to work a great deal to realize their intellectual or professional ambitions and in whose life there has been, as a result, very little room for love. As a general rule a man has attained the goal of his ambition by the middle forties. His *libido* then begins to flow in the direction of what he too much neglected in his youth. The famous "noon-day devil" is not just the creation of a novelist's imagination. The psychoanalyst is in a position to enable us to understand it in a deeper way than the novelist.

There would also seem to be a greater susceptibility for love during certain seasons of the year—in the springtime, for example. Joy of life is at its most intense at that time of year and the affective life then quite normally dominates everything else. That is why it seems to me that the beginning of summer is a very poor time to hold examinations in colleges and universities. The majority of young people certainly would succeed much better during the winter when their affective life is only half awake.

Whatever the seasons and the periods of life, and whatever may be an individual's ego-ideal, it is evident that chance plays a great role in the birth of love. A certain person whom today we hardly notice because we are preoccupied with our health, professional cares or intellectual problems, could be recognized as the most perfect embodiment of our ego-ideal if met at a time when our psychic energy is better disposed. We can fall in love with such an individual on the spot.

Love at first sight is something that actually occurs. Love can hit a person as suddenly as a thunderbolt. Even then, however, the subject has to be in a state of susceptibility for it, and if love at first sight is to be reciprocal, both subjects have to find themselves in this favorably disposed state. It would be a mistake, however, to expect that love develops exclusively in this sudden way. Frequently, it insinuates itself into the hearts of two individuals without their perceiving its presence. A man and a woman may have known each other since childhood without ever having experienced any particular attraction for each other, and without ever having given a thought to the fact that they could be anything except "good friends." Then one day, perhaps when they are no longer altogether young, they may discover they are deeply in love with each other and have been so, perhaps, for quite a long time.

Martha and Anthony had lived as neighbors and good friends for the first twenty years of their lives. Events subsequently separated them. Each of them had married someone else, and neither had heard of the other again. One day, when both of them were in their forties, they met by chance in a museum. Immediately it was a case of a great, imperious love. It caused them to break the ties that until then they had considered indestructible. Life apart from each other appeared to be henceforth unthinkable.

Neither Martha nor Anthony has been psychoanalyzed. It is not possible, therefore, to provide any certain interpretation of their belated sudden falling in love. Why had neither of them recognized sooner that the other represented the perfect realization of their respective ego-ideals? Was it their youthful distractions? Had they grown mutually complementary only during the long years of separation and precisely as a result of what each of them had acquired through their respective love of another? Had they always been in love with each other without knowing it? It is difficult to answer these questions just as it is difficult (if not impossible) to answer the majority of questions raised by the beginning of any love whatever. Too many factors in the realm of affectivity still elude our categories, even our psychoanalytic ones. The majority of cases of which we have exhaustive knowledge are cases involving neurotics. The psychologist has to resist the temptation to interpret normal cases in the light of what he knows about the abnormal.

3. Choices Based on Complexes

Certain people's choice of a partner strike those outside the domain of depth psychology as completely scandalous. It is not a rare occurrence for a pretty, much-sought-after woman to fall in love with a man who is sickly, an invalid, puny, or ugly. It is whispered sometimes that such men are endowed with exceptional sexual prowess and that this is the reason certain "vicious" women show a preference for them. There is not the slightest experimental proof for such an explanation. In many instances, the woman has settled her choice on the man in question prior to any sexual experience with him.

Colette, twenty-six, a pretty college professor of literature, showed herself so averse to advances made to her by men that some of her colleagues thought she had lesbian tendencies. To everybody's surprise, it was learned one day that there was a liaison between this brilliant young intellectual and a very minor employee, who was somewhat sickly and altogether devoid of charm. She was in love with him.

In the course of the therapy to which Colette had recourse several years later, it was revealed that her strong personality had experienced great difficulty in asserting itself during adolescence when she found herself caught between a tyrannical father and older brothers who always treated her as "a little girl." Later on as a student, she found occasion to satisfy her aptitude for leadership in protecting weaker persons. She directed an organization of young women with great success and took enormous pleasure in being able to experience her own strength. But this afforded her only partial satisfaction. What her unconscious needed, to erase the humiliation inflicted by her father and brothers on the little girl she had been, was to dominate a man and become his protector. That is why she instinctively treated with coldness and disdain any man she thought might behave toward her the way the men in her childhood had, asserting his intellectual or physical superiority over her. This is also the reason she fell in love with a man she knew she was superior to in every way, and who needed to be protected and helped by her. Before her psychotherapy, Colette was completely unaware of the existence of such a complex in her emotional make-up. She had been content to state that strong, brilliant men "just did not speak to her," and that she liked a man who was neither strong nor brilliant.

Elsa, the daughter of a wealthy industrialist, had experienced an exceptionally unhappy childhood and adolescence. She was still a child when her parents were divorced. Both of them remarried. The little girl lived sometimes with her mother and at other times with her father. She did not feel she had a home with either of them. Her half-brothers and half-sisters on both sides looked upon her as an intruder. When she was still fairly young, it was in the arms of men that she began to look for the affection, the lack of which had made her so miserable. She was too avid for love, however, and always got "carried away" too quickly. This led to one disappointment after another. During the war she met a young officer who fell in love with her. He was a handsome and intelligent young man who belonged to a well-known aristocratic family. For the first time in her life, Elsa knew what it meant to be truly loved. She naturally did not refuse him when he asked her to marry him. She bore her title of countess proudly, almost arrogantly. It seemed to her that Providence at last had avenged her. Other women envied her good fortune, and everyone thought she was perfectly happy.

One day, however, several years after her marriage, the scandal broke. Her husband and his entire entourage in high society found out that Elsa had been the mistress of her poor, émigré chauffeur for quite some time. She confessed to her husband that even in the beginning of their marriage she had betrayed him with some of the servants and liverymen. By contrast, she always rejected with proud and sincere indignation the advances made to her by men belonging to the same social group as her husband.

Elsa's amorous adventures seemed "monstrous" to her husband. He was ready to forgive her, but only on the condition that she go to see a psychoanalyst.

Elsa's behavior, in the main, was not that of a neurotic individual. She did not experience any anxiety. She had no "complex" other than a deep sense of inferiority resulting from her unhappy childhood, and more particularly from a refusal of love on the part of her father. On the conscious level, she considered her marriage, and the new social position she acquired along with it, as precious compensations for past humiliations. As for her arrogance, it was nothing more than an awkward manifestation of her ardent desire to convince herself—more than to convince others—of her "success." In reality, she felt completely ill at ease in her new situation. The refinement of the way of life of her husband's family and associates was too much for her. It constantly reminded her of her Cinderella role. In the arms of her husband, more than anywhere else perhaps, she felt humiliated and inferior. This made it impossible for her to enjoy any of the pleasures of love. She interpreted her husband's affection as condescension. She said that she respected and loved her husband, and that she owed him a great debt of gratitude for having chosen to marry her. But her feeling of gratitude existed only on the conscious level. Her unconscious, steeped in guilt feelings, looked upon him as a "sorry type" for having married a girl like herself.

In the course of analysis, Elsa recalled that even before her marriage she had never succeeded in finding any pleasure in the company of men whom she knew were socially or intellectually her superior. She had never been happy except in the arms of men of humble station, men who considered it an honor to be permitted to make love to her. She had to be able to experience generosity, condescension and a feeling of protectiveness toward the men who made love to her.

These antecedent circumstances make Elsa's passion for her chauffeur, the last in time and the humblest of all her lovers, perfectly understandable. She never felt more like a countess than when she was in his arms, while she had the impression she was being made fun of when she was addressed by that title in society. As proud as she was of the material and social position she had attained through her marriage, she stated at the beginning of therapy that she was prepared to abandon everything and go off with her chauffeur to live in poverty and social disgrace.

By degrees, in the course of treatment, Elsa became conscious of the unauthentic, neurotic character of her love for the chauffeur. Feeling herself morally crushed by the aristocratic character of her husband and his family, for her unconscious it was a means of rejecting their domination to prevent herself from experiencing an orgasm in the arms of her husband. The unconscious desire to get revenge for the humiliations she so often experienced had played an important role in her sudden love-struck feelings toward her chauffeur. She was not unaware of the fact that she was inflicting humiliation on those she looked upon as her enemies by being the young countess of X who was the mistress of a man in such a lowly position. Moreover, while Elsa seemed consciously to want to keep her affair secret, her unconscious behaved in a remarkably clever way to insure that the scandal would see the light of day.

It is true that Elsa's emotional position in regard to her father also played a great role with respect to the impossibility of her experiencing any pleasure with "superior" men, whom she unconsciously identified with him. It is not pertinent to the subject matter of the present chapter to develop this theme, however. I shall content myself with pointing out the fact that after her inferiority complex was resolved in therapy and her feelings toward her father normalized, Elsa became capable of loving her husband even in a physical way. She also discovered that it is not only men in lowly walks of life who expect generosity and protectiveness from a woman they love; she found out that the superior man also needs them.

It would be easy to describe numerous cases in which more or less seriously neurotic complexes are at the source of experiences of sudden love. This would be true even in the case of individuals who cannot be classified strictly as neurotic. However, the two cases just presented (as well as those that could be added to them) do not authorize us to establish any theory about sudden love which could be called "scientific" in the precise sense in which a theory in mathematics or physics can be called scientific. When we speak of psychological laws, we must never forget that none of them possesses the same universal character and the same rigorous applications as the laws of the other sciences.

In each "case" one encounters factors of a strictly individual nature, to which any psychologist worthy of the name has to pay at least as much attention as he does to factors that seem to fit in with his theories.

The two cases discussed nevertheless permit us to draw one conclusion. In a number of women, the choice of a partner in love is influenced by an unconscious revolt against their inferiority as a woman. It is impossible for them to love any man they cannot dominate and take a protective attitude toward. We saw this complex at work in the case of a superior woman like Colette, but also in a humiliated woman like Elsa. Only a woman who is perfectly reconciled with her femininity is in a position to love without her unconscious using it as a means to express her resentment over her biological, sociological and psychological condition of being a woman. With unerring instinct, her heart is directed toward a man who is capable of protecting her and who has need of her affection. While the woman with a complex experiences the position she is generally obliged to adopt in physical love as a domination and a humiliation, the "normal" woman wants to experience it as a symbol of the protection afforded her by the one she loves.

We have been discussing choices based on complexes as they are encountered among women. It should not be deduced from what has been said that such choices are to be found exclusively among representatives of the "second sex." Unconscious motives of a more or less neurotic character can have just as much influence on the amorous choices of men. Here again, of course, general theory runs the risk of being contradicted by certain individual cases.

Everyone is familiar with cases of weak and timid "mama's boys" who can fall in love only with strong, aggressive women or with virile women of decisive and energetic character. Their unconscious thus directs them toward women who will take the place of a protective, dominating mother. Many "mother hens," or as Freud called them, "castrating mothers," have no idea of the disappointments in love for which they are preparing their sons.

When a "mama's boy" suddenly falls in love with a petite, fragile woman who is timid and indecisive, however, it cannot be deduced too readily that a castrating mother has exercised no influence at all on his choice. The chances are he wants to get revenge. With regard to a woman who is weaker than himself, he may be attempting to dominate and protect his mother, with whom his unconscious identifies his wife or mistress. Weak men of this sort, unconsciously revolting against maternal tyranny, stand a very good chance of making ridiculous domestic tyrants out of themselves, to the great sorrow of their wife and children.

In the case of both men and women, the choice of a partner that is motivated by an unconscious neurotic complex always carries along with it a number of serious disadvantages. It is the source of the greater majority of misfortunes and catastrophes that befall love. It is undesirable for future husbands and wives to be satisfied with a pre-marital examination that is restricted to matters pertaining to physical health. They should also seek clarification about their psychological situation. In this way they could save themselves a great deal of trouble. Emotional infantilism is actually the principal reason why the choice of a partner is seldom very free—in spite of appearances.

It rarely happens (except in certain Russian novels) that an individual falls in love only once in his lifetime. It is a fact that the same individual is capable of choosing a succession of partners on the basis of conscious and unconscious motives that are different every time. The more a person becomes a distinct individual the more complex the human psyche.

Andrew first felt the pangs of love when he was sixteen. The object of his love was a friend of his mother's who was his mother's age. A desire to be emancipated from his mother's possessive affection entered into his choice, but so did his need to continue to enjoy its benefits from a substitute whom he could, moreover, tyrannize over as he pleased. Later on there was a long period in Andrew's life during which he chased one pretty girl after another, all of them of the timid or shy type. Unconsciously, he was constantly seeking to convince himself of his powers of seduction. He was trying in this way to overcome an inferiority complex, a lack of confidence in himself which was the result of a severe illness he had suffered during adolescence. Finally, at thirty-five, he fell in love with a woman in whom he recognized his equal in character and intelligence. With her he was able to experience a real person-to-person communion. So he married her.

CHAPTER THREE

PLATONIC LOVE

LITTLE RESPONSIBILITY or credit belongs to the philosopher Plato for the respective failures and successes encountered with the type of love that is commonly designated "platonic." Love that aspires to be purely "ideal," that wants to have nothing to do with the body and particularly not with sexuality, has come to be called platonic simply on the basis of the fact that Plato considered eternal ideas to be more "true" than tangible realities, and developed a philosophy which has a general tendency to envision a radical opposition between body and soul.

1. *The Loves of Children and Adolescents*

Platonic love is most often and most naturally encountered among children. I am not referring to the famous Oedipus complex—the love of the small child for one of his parents. The foundation for the Freudian ideas on this subject will be discussed in a later chapter. It is enough at this point to observe that to the extent to which the Oedipus situation exists, it is a question of an unconscious desire of a sexual nature. The "platonic love" presently to be discussed is something completely different in character.

I have rarely observed true love among children before the age of ten. It is true that children of five or six talk about marrying someone and designate one of their little playmates as their "fiancé." Generally, however, this is simply a matter of echoing the conversation and joking of adults. Friendships among little children imply sentiments of a very different nature from that of love, even platonic love.

As I pointed out in the first chapter, between the ages of ten and fourteen (the pre-pubertal period) sexual impulses and emotional reactions are generally divorced from each other. A boy simply experiences an emotional need to love and—to a lesser degree—to be loved. He often tries to have sexual contact with little girls or sometimes with other boys, or even with animals. As a general rule, however, there is no emotional affection involved. Quite the contrary. All the boys of this age whom I know display great scorn for the little girl who lets them "touch" her. Infinitely less than the adult is the child willing to acknowledge the equality of the sexes.

Sentiments of platonic love are met with among children in two very different forms. They are directed either to a distant, ideal person who is absolutely inaccessible, or to a person who is near and known, but whom the child himself exaggeratedly idealizes.

Eleven-year-old Paul was hopelessly in love with Greta Garbo, the most celebrated movie-star of that time. He never failed to see each of her films several times. Before going to sleep at night he lovingly contemplated the actress's photographs and put a penny under his pillow in the hope of thus increasing his chances of dreaming about her while he was asleep. He wrote her ardent love letters, inspired more by the novels he read than by an analysis of his own feelings. Paul experienced no desire, however, to make his love known to his beloved. He was content to show the letters he wrote to his best friend, who also shared his passion for the actress. There was no jealousy between the two friends. As an adult, Paul recalled that there was absolutely no desire, not even the vaguest sexual image, connected with his love for Greta Garbo. His dreams of her, like his thoughts, were completely "pure." It is true that at that particular age he commenced to "touch" himself, but in doing so he is certain that his excitation was aroused by images that bore no relation at all to his love.

The passion for Greta Garbo lasted for about a year. Little by little, almost imperceptibly, a classmate of his own age was substituted for the actress in his dreams and thoughts. Lisa was not someone inaccessible. Paul imagined himself taking a walk with her to the bank of the river. Sometimes he dreamed of their marriage ceremony. She was his "fiancée." He wrote love letters to her also. While he never sent them, he would never show these letters to anyone. For some unknown reason, a sense of shame prevented him from sharing his feelings for Lisa with his friend.

Before he discovered that he was in love with her, Paul had had excellent relations with Lisa. They were the two best students in the class; they played together during recreation, borrowed each other's books, and sometimes did their homework together. The young girl did not understand why the attitude of her friend had changed so suddenly. He avoided her. He didn't speak to her any longer except to sneer at her. And she was the only one to whom this well brought up and naturally sensitive boy sometimes addressed coarse words. (He recalled that it was especially on a day after his most tender dreams that he couldn't help doing something mean to Lisa.) It is true that Paul himself did not understand, any more than Lisa did, his hostile behavior toward the one to whom he wanted to speak with tender and passionate words as the lovers in his bedside books spoke. Why did he behave this way toward the one he dreamed of serving as the knights in the romances he read served their fair lady? His most ardent desire was to make Lisa admire him, but now he had every reason to fear that she would detest him!

The psychologist has no difficulty in understanding the contradiction between Paul's feelings and his behavior. He was employing a well-known defense mechanism. In his unconscious, the boy was afraid of his ardent love. So long as its object was an inaccessible star, there could be no danger. Lisa, however, was very near at hand, and therefore constituted a threat to the boy's youthful autonomy. Consequently, he had to make her as distant as the famous actress. Hence his aggressive behavior in her regard. Secretly, he never stopped observing his beloved. He followed her as closely as he could on the street, imagining to himself how she might find herself exposed to serious dangers, and how he would save her at the peril of his life. She would then understand how much he loved her, and would forgive him for his meanness. When he caught her talking to other friends, all of them nicer to her than he was, he suffered all the pangs of jealousy.

It was not until three years later, at a time when he had scarcely thought of her in several months, that Paul sent his first love letter to Lisa. Both of them were by this time fifteen years old. Sending the letter seemed to him such a terrible audacity that the next day he was so embarrassed he didn't dare go to school. However, Lisa answered his letter. From that time on, and for several years, the two young people loved each other. They took walks together hand in hand to deserted places, read the same books, and wrote impassioned letters to each other during vacations. No sexual desire seems to have troubled their platonic love, even after Paul had known several gallant adventures. Twenty years later, Paul still thought with tenderness of the girl he considered his first love, classifying his feelings for Greta Garbo as simply childish. It pained him to believe that *his* Lisa could have known the embraces of love, although he knew she was married and the mother of several children. Paul was not sexually inhibited. He considered sexual pleasure to be perfectly licit—even necessary—for all other women. Lisa alone was the exception. She symbolized the ideal of purity and the ethereal beauty of his childhood.

Not all childhood loves, however, are so completely platonic as the love between Lisa and Paul.

Caroline, a young girl of fifteen with all the romanticism characteristic of her age, loved her cousin, who was five years older than she. She idealized in an extreme way this young man who seemed to be quite ordinary. She fondly identified him with the epic heroes. Her strong budding sensuality even caused her sometimes to imagine him as taking her in his arms and kissing her, as she had often seen it done in films. Caroline had only the vaguest ideas about sexual relations. From her reading and the conversations of adults she had overheard, however, she knew that men visited prostitutes for the purpose of "making love." Sometimes she observed streetwalkers with mixed feelings of shame and envy. On certain nights in bed, when the need for love made itself felt very strongly, she imagined herself disguised as a prostitute and walking the street. Her beloved cousin arrives, but doesn't recognize her in the dark. She is about to come to know "love" with him. Her imagination did not dare to make the situation more precise.

One day, in the absence of her parents, Caroline's cousin visited her. He kissed her on the mouth and tried to caress her. After those imaginary debauches, one might think the young girl would be very happy. But that would be a mistake. She defended herself, slapped the young man's face, and then furiously washed her mouth, which had been "soiled" by his kiss. From that day on, she was no longer in love with her cousin. In spite of her imaginary debauches it seems that Caroline's love had been as completely platonic as Paul's and Lisa's.

The loves of children and adolescents deserve to be taken as seriously as the loves of adults and older men and women. The affective life is coextensive with existence. One can love passionately at any age. Even before the sexual instinct matures, the child needs to love, and himself loves in an affective way. It also happens that after sexual impulses have become extinguished an older person again falls in love.

It is obviously not my point to maintain that the sexual impulse has no connection with the platonic loves of childhood. The simple fact that in the vast majority of these cases such loves are of a heterosexual nature is enough to establish the contrary. In platonic love, however, it is a matter of sex in the broad sense, with no conscious link to what can be termed genital. It seems that emotional maturing and genital maturing follow parallel courses, and that before they achieve their successful fusion, the genital and the emotional go their separate ways. Undoubtedly the many strict prohibitions that surround sexuality in almost all civilizations render the union of love and sexuality the more difficult. Even in the most advanced circles, it is a rare educator who succeeds in not casting discredit on matters of a sexual nature. There are things about which it is forbidden to speak, shameful things, therefore. The child who "touches himself," or "touches" another child, is punished without any explanation. The priest in confession seldom fails to ask questions about "dirty" thoughts and actions. In the face of this general reprobation of the impulses which he feels stirring in his flesh, the child reads books which give him a very elevated and pure idea of love. But there is no need of books for the feelings of tenderness and admiration which the child or the adolescent experiences for the person he loves to be made pure and noble. Instinctively, he keeps the shameful and the sinful out of them—that is to say, he excludes sexuality from them.

In the vast majority of cases there is no difficulty in childhood loves remaining platonic. Little by little, and notwithstanding all the prohibitions, the integration of sexuality and affectivity will be effected all the same. In spite of everything, the general tendency in modern education is in the direction of lessening sexual tabus, if not eliminating them completely. Among those who are predisposed to become neurotic, however, the condemnation attached to sexuality and the exaggerated idealization of love more or less seriously risk compromising their adult love-life.

2. Good and Bad Faith in Platonic Love

Platonic love also exists among adults. It is appropriate here to make a careful distinction between platonic love in good faith and platonic love in bad faith, it being understood, naturally, that bad faith is generally only on the unconscious level.

Louise, a woman of thirty-five, was married for fifteen years. She told me enthusiastically about her "completely platonic" love for Albert, her husband's best friend. For quite some time her husband had no longer been able to satisfy Louise's emotional needs. Considering herself very idealistic, a very "superior type of woman," she reproached her husband for being too earthy and prosaic, a person with whom it was not possible to speak about anything except the most ordinary things of everyday life—the children, money, his job—to the point of monotonous regularity. She was frigid. But instead of finding anything wrong with that, on the contrary, she viewed it as a confirmation of her character as a woman interested only in the noble things of the spirit.

In Albert, she maintained, she had met the perfect companion of her dreams. They spent long hours together, playing music, reading poetry, enjoying the ecstasy of beautiful landscapes viewed against the setting sun. She was absolutely certain there was no sexual desire, nothing sensual at all in this love. Albert had satisfactory sexual relations with his wife, and she herself experienced not the slightest temptation to betray her husband for something which she "valued so little." Nevertheless, the two "platonic" lovers held hands when they were alone and recently they had begun to kiss each other "lightly" on the lips. Louise asserted, however, that neither of them experienced any sensual emotion. These were simply token manifestations of their tender feeling for each other.

On the conscious level, Louise was certainly sincere when she spoke about the strictly platonic character of her feelings for Albert. Since I have never had the occasion to meet him personally, I have no more reason for suspecting his sincerity than I have for suspecting Louise's, especially if it is true that he had never betrayed his wife. Anyone who understands the unconscious mechanisms of the psyche, however, will hesitate to consider the love between Louise and Albert genuinely platonic. If it were, one would have to conclude that he was presented with two very exceptional human beings, both of whom were endowed with a very strong capacity for sublimation. In the absence of proof, the psychologist will consider this love to be no more platonic than the love of the many engaged couples who desire to remain "pure" until marriage. The only difference is that Louise and Albert intended to remain chaste "fiancés" forever. A few weeks later Louise confided in me, however, that she had become her lover's mistress. This was something, of course, that could be foreseen.

Persons who aspire to platonic love confidently point to examples of certain famous pairs: Clare and Francis of Assisi, Teresa of Avila and John of the Cross, Jeanne de Chantal and Francis de Sales, and others.

Speaking only of these three saintly pairs, and allowing for obvious differences among them, I think one has the right to call the relationship between them a relationship of love, in spite of the fact that they themselves undoubtedly would be opposed to any such designation. Their love was obviously the most perfect form of platonic love, in the sense that nothing sexual was involved in the affection they had for each other. In trying to take them as examples, one must not lose sight of the fact that they were saints, that these were very great mystics. They had no need, either consciously or unconsciously, to repress their sexuality, since it found itself completely sublimated in their immense love of each other in God. No unconscious bad faith vitiated the platonic character of their love. It is sufficient to reflect on what these men and women were, however, to conclude that no one, not even relatively "spiritualized" persons, can pretend to be able to imitate them.

The only cases of successful platonic love that I have seen are to be found among older lovers.

Christian, forty-five years of age and married, had fallen in love with his secretary, Marcelle, a young girl of twenty-five. Mutually struck by the darts of love, they soon became lovers. After the initial intoxication had subsided both of them realized the "impossibility" of the situation in which they found themselves. They were both deeply religious and loyal persons. An ambiguous way of life was intolerable for them. Besides, Christian was very much attached to his children, and although he no longer loved his wife, he recognized his obligations to her, which were impossible for him to renounce. The two lovers agreed to sublimate their love and keep it platonic. In the first six months or so, they failed two or three times to keep their resolution, but finally their efforts were crowned with success. For nearly ten years now, their love has become so clearly platonic that even the temptation to sexuality is absent.

Since I know of several similar cases, I believe I have a right to think that, under such conditions, platonic love can actually exist. It can only exist, however, between two persons who live on a high spiritual plane, and between whom there is a sufficiently intense spiritual communion.

3. Platonic Love in Neurotics

The love of Louise and Albert was a case of platonic love based unconsciously on bad faith. The case of Christian and Marcelle, after sublimation, was an instance of platonic love in good faith. There is yet a third category of adult platonic lovers. There is a form of platonic love which exists in the case of those whose emotional development is arrested in some infantile fixation.

There are some persons who love in a platonic way all their lives, in the manner of children. Not only do they make no attempt to yield to true love, but they are actually afraid of it. They categorically refuse it and flee from it when it is offered to them.

This type of love is found more frequently among women than men, although the latter are not completely immune from it. As was pointed out before in the case of children, the object of such love is a person who is distant and inaccessible. This is precisely the way in which it is possible to distinguish platonic love that is pathological in character from the type of platonic love described in the foregoing section, which—in spite of everything—is nevertheless normal. In the normal case of platonic love, it is a matter of two persons, present to each other and, in good or bad faith, constrained to love each other without any participation in their love on the part of the body.

Julia, forty years of age and married for eighteen years, was not in love with her husband. She accused him of knowing nothing about love, and of having married her just for the sake of having a woman at his disposal for his "piggish desires." From adolescence on, she had never ceased to dream of a love that would be absolutely pure. She could not conceive how love could be anything but spiritual. She regretted bitterly and was ashamed of not being able to remain completely frigid in the arms of her husband. Her own sensual transports humiliated and vilified her in her own eyes. She had love and esteem only for exceptional persons with whom she had no direct contact: a famous lecturer, a writer whose books she admired, a doctor who gave medical care (not to herself, but to her children); or again, some movie actor or ballet dancer. Her platonic love often changed its object, but the fervor of it each time was just as great as if she had remained fourteen years old. Her drawers were full of ardent love letters which she had written to successive objects of her devotion—naturally without ever having mailed them. She spent many hours dreaming of the replies she would have received if she had sent the letters, and some replies she had even written herself. She could never imagine—it could not be possible—that these "superior" men ever indulged any "piggish desires" the way her too earthy husband did. In her dreams and daytime reveries, she imagined them holding her hand, or she saw herself seated on their lap "like a little girl sitting on her father's knee." If there was any kissing, it was only on the head, always the way one kissed a little girl. She generally saw herself in her dreams as a little girl.

Julia had been very strongly attached to her father during her childhood and adolescence. He was a rough and abrupt man who rarely displayed any tenderness toward her. He obviously preferred her older sister, who was less emotional and less "complicated" than she. But Julia's love found an added stimulus in this indifference of her father, and she would no longer be able to love anyone except someone who was distant and inaccessible. Her father was, and remained, her ideal man, someone who could be adored from afar, the way one adores God. That her father could have done anything "dirty" seemed unbelievable to her. "Of course," she thought, "since my mother did have three children, my father must have slept with her. It is hard for me to believe it, however. At any rate, he must have done so only three times, in order to have us—myself and my brother and sister. Even a noble man," she added, by way of excusing him, "can have his rare moments of weakness, which one has to learn to forgive."

In marrying the man who was "offered" to her, she had a vague hope that her relations with him would not be like those she actually had had with her father, but like those she had wished to have with him. She was fully aware that in marriage she would have to have children, but she refused to let herself have any clear idea about the way in which one goes about having them. Her admiration for her husband ceased from the marriage night on. She could no longer do anything but detest him. Little by little, her affective life began to have recourse to seeking its nourishment in the guise of platonic loves, whom she infallibly selected on the basis of their being as inaccessible as her father, whom she loved so much.

Platonic love as exemplified in the case of Julia is obviously neurotic in structure. To become capable of loving in a normal, adult manner, she had to undergo lengthy psychotherapy. As a result of therapy, it became possible for her to normalize her feelings for her father, who long since had been deceased. Admitting that her father was certainly a man worthy of the esteem and admiration of his daughter, but not on the score of his being a stranger to the common condition of humanity, she no longer demanded the "superhuman" either from her husband or from herself.

In contrast to Julia, the majority of women who experience platonic love for men who are inaccessible are absolutely frigid in their sexual relations with their husband or lover. Sometimes it is precisely their neurotic inaptitude for sexual love which causes them to desire a love that is "ideal." At other times they are frigid because they idealize the notion of love in a disproportionate way. This too has a more or less neurotic motivation for its foundation.

Not so long ago, certain confessors and spiritual directors admired and praised platonic love. They spoke of physical love as a concession to the weakness of the flesh and enthusiastically recommended to the young Christians they were forming examples of the virginal marriages practiced by certain saints. Between the two wars, a veritable epidemic of "white marriages" raged in a large sector of Catholic university circles until the principal theoretician and apostle of the cult himself married, and in a way that was completely contrary to the rules!

It was pointed out before that in certain exceptional cases platonic love can be considered something not only tolerable but even recommendable. This is true, however, only when there is no question of a neurotic refusal to face reality, but instead the love is the fruit of genuine sublimation.

Two people can love each other, although sexual love may be forbidden them for certain valid reasons of an objective or a subjective nature. One could ask them to renounce their love, and that generally is what moralists do. But the psychologist knows of many cases in which such a destruction of love would seem worse than suicide, their love having become the reason for living and the stimulus to activity for the two partners. It can also happen that lovers, instead of following the advice to renounce love, will break with everything that constitutes an obstacle to their love—family ties, religion, and so on.

Leaving aside the completely exceptional cases of the saints, it must be admitted that the realization of platonic love is obviously a difficult matter. It is one that is fraught with many dangers, even for persons who are both capable and desirous of sublimation. I have known any number of cases in which the results have been totally lamentable. It remains true, nevertheless, that such a form of love is not to be condemned a priori. Intelligent priests and experienced psychologists can be of real help to devout people and with people generally. There are good chances of success for candidates for platonic love, provided it is not a question of neurosis, but of sublimation.

When platonic love is the fruit of a neurotic sexual repression, however, one should never encourage it. It can only result in inhibitions for the subject himself and it can often do great harm to others. This type of love must be remedied through the elimination of emotional infantilism, and this is a task which psychotherapy alone is competent to accomplish.

Those men, and especially those women, who love a distant person in a platonic manner, almost never find it desirable to be in the presence of their idol. As a matter of fact, such lovers generally show themselves incapable of the least resistance to the advances of their beloved, and such advances stand a good chance of being in no way platonic.

Isabelle belonged to a family and a social circle that was traditionally very Christian. She had been taught to consider her virginity her highest virtue, and that the loss of it would dishonor her forever. Very pretty, she had been the object of a good deal of masculine homage, but at the age of twenty-seven she had allowed only one man even to go so far as to kiss her. She had to safeguard the "flower" of her virginity in all its integrity for her future husband.

Isabelle was in love—at a distance—with a famous writer whom she had never seen, but whose books she had admired for a long time. For several years she had written him impassioned letters, but the feelings she expressed in them were, in her mind, absolutely platonic. Never having experienced any sexual desire, she had difficulty imagining that it was possible to love in any other way.

One day she had the occasion to go to the town where her idol lived. She obtained permission for an interview with him. After half an hour of conversation about subjects of an esthetic nature, she stood up to take her leave. Touched perhaps by the devotion the young girl displayed toward him, the writer kissed her on the lips. Not only did she accept his kiss, but she threw herself into his arms and allowed herself, without resistance, to be deprived of the virginity which had seemed so precious to her. It was not that she was overwhelmed by a sudden sexual passion. It was simply that she had accustomed herself over a long period of time to the thought that from Lim she could expect only the sublime.

There are also cases of women who love the man they admire in a platonic way, and who would never give themselves to him in a sexual manner; at the same time they readily give themselves to a man who has no prestige in their eyes. This is a specific consequence of the disdain for sexual matters which exists in certain social circles.

CHAPTER FOUR

LOVE AND INCEST

ACCORDING TO the opinion of certain Freudians (which is not to be confused with the doctrine of Freud himself), everyone's first love is always incestuous in character. If a modern Molière wanted to ridicule the spirit of systematization to the point of caricature, he would find no subject that would lend itself better to his purpose than the notoriously famous Oedipus complex, which plays the role of a real *deus ex machina* in Freudian psychoanalysis.

1. The Oedipus Complex

Let us recall the legend. The oracle has predicted that Laius, King of Thebes, would be killed by his own son. The king decides to kill Oedipus to prevent this from happening. He pins his infant son to a tree, leaving him there to die. Oedipus is saved by shepherds who take him to Polybius, King of Corinth. There he is given a princely education. Oedipus meets Laius later when he has become a man, but he does not know that he is his father. In a scuffle between them, Oedipus kills Laius, thus bringing to pass what the oracle had predicted. After solving the riddle of the Sphinx and freeing the city of Thebes, Oedipus becomes its king. In accordance with custom, he marries Jocasta, the widow of his predecessor, not realizing she is his own mother. Jocasta hangs herself when apprised of the facts through an oracle. Oedipus tears out his eyes and departs from Thebes with his daughter Antigone. He disappears mysteriously into the groves of the Eumenides in Attica.

This legend which has been the source of inspiration for so many dramatists, is for Freud the symbolic expression of a psychological drama common to all men. On the conscious level, it is true that Oedipus is unaware

76

of the fact that he is killing his own father and marrying his own mother. It is not, however, by chance that he does so. The real character perpetrating the trick is the unconscious, which is not at all ignorant of the true situation. Unconsciously, it is really his father whom Oedipus hates and desires to murder, and for the precise purpose of being able to marry his mother. Oedipus has always been in love with her. He loves her with a sexual love. His father therefore appears before him with all the characteristics of a rival. The same situation exists in the case of all other men. Although their love and rivalry do not have to result in incest and murder in the literal sense of the terms, all men are incestuous and are parricides in the depths of their psyche. It is not difficult to understand why the theory of the Oedipus complex, presented in this way, created such a scandal.

As for girls, their first love is also an incestuous one. In their case, it is the father who is the object of love and the mother whom they hate as rival.

There is no need to turn to psychoanalysis to realize that there is such a thing as incestuous love. There is no need to mention that there are socially and morally corrupt environments in which a drunken father may violate his own daughter, or brothers and sisters may be obliged to share the same bed—not only during their childhood, but sometimes even during adolescence and right up until the time they are married. If they happen to have sexual relations under such circumstances, it is usually almost in spite of themselves. Besides, in such cases, it is hardly possible to speak of love in the sense we have given this word in the first chapter. But there are situations of a much more characteristic nature, in which sociological conditions do not enter as an influence, but which are specifically psychological in nature.

Dominique's father was high up in government service. He came from a family belonging to the upper middle class. When I first met Dominique, she had already completed her studies at the university. All the members of the family were practicing Catholics, and the family enjoyed an excellent reputation. Dominique had always been very much attached to her father. She recalled that it was when she was about fifteen years old that she began to experience her first sensual difficulties. It was when her father would hug her, or when his hands—probably inadvertently—might touch her body. She saw no harm in it. It seemed inconceivable to her that her father, whom she so much admired, could do anything that was not perfectly right. By degrees, however, her father's caresses became more deliberate, and he began to kiss his daughter on the mouth. Far from displaying any annoyance at this, she sought the paternal caresses and kisses and often took the initiative herself with respect to them. She was eighteen when—"through my fault," she said—the relations between her and her father became clearly erotic, even though they never developed to the point of complete consummation.

Dominique and her father were very conscious of the fact that what they were doing was not right. They went to confession, resolved not to start all over again, kept their good resolution for a few weeks or a few months, and then fell again. This situation went on for several years, until the time when the young girl found herself in love with another man. Even then, however, the break with her father was not altogether complete. She thought little about him, and at times she experienced real hatred toward him, but for nearly two years more her feelings toward him remained very ambivalent. Dominique had to undergo a slow process of emotional maturing before she could find herself in the position of adopting a mode of filial behavior toward her father that was somewhat more normal.

In order to interpret this incestuous love adequately from the psychological point of view, it is necessary to become familiar not only with the unconscious psyche of Dominique, but also with that of her father. It appears that his wife's repression of any kind of erotic feeling—due probably to misguided piety—was at the root of the intimacy this man was looking for with his daughter. By degrees, almost unconsciously, an attraction that had formerly been platonic took on a sexual character. Undoubtedly he also desired to become disentangled from her, and he regretted bitterly the harm he was doing his daughter. The condition of emotional frustration in which he lived with his wife, however, made it practically impossible for him to detach himself from his sexual attraction to his daughter. He also seems to have had a very strong sense of the fact that, once his daughter had been liberated from her sexual passion, she would only despise him.

As for Dominique, nothing gives us the right to presume that in the beginning her strong attachment for her father was anything other than the normal preference a girl shows for her father. As a matter of fact, such a preference seems to be almost universal, particularly in the case of the eldest daughter who has many brothers and sisters. Elsewhere[1] we have pointed out that it could only have been an excessive spirit of systematization that allowed Freud (and particularly his disciples) to view such an attachment of a girl for her father, or of a boy for his mother, as sexual in nature—even in the broad sense of the term. To return to Dominique, it happened that in her case the awakening of a very strong sensuality coincided with puberty. She sought the company of boys, and willingly permitted herself to be kissed and caressed by them. However, very strict family discipline made it extremely difficult for her to have contact with young people. Visitors seldom came to the house, and she was never permitted to go out alone in the evening. This undoubtedly is the explanation of the fact that (without at first being conscious of its erotic character) she sought the satisfactions she had been prohibited from trying to find elsewhere from her tyrant-father himself. It is for the moralists to decide whether or not it would have been better for Dominique's emotional maturity if she had enjoyed greater liberty in her relationships outside the family. As a psychologist, I think it was in large part due precisely to the imposition of too many prohibitions that the awakening of sexuality took on an almost obsessive character in the case of this young girl.

The case of André was fundamentally no different from that of Dominique. His mother was a famous actress, who was divorced and lived for a long time alone with her only son. Cruelly frustrated and deceived by a husband incapable of understanding her, she diverted all of her great need for affection toward her son. The main purpose of her life was to make of him a man absolutely different from his father. André slept in the twin bed next to his mother's: that is to say, in the bed hardly ever occupied by her husband. His mother applied herself to

[1] *Clartés et ténèbres de l'âme,* chap. VIII.

the task of forming the sensibility and esthetic taste of her son. Contrary to good sense, she encouraged him to pursue an artistic career even though (in the judgment of an impartial third party) he had only mediocre talents. As one might expect, because of this extremely jealous maternal love, André adapted poorly to social life and made hardly any friends for himself. His conduct toward young girls was characterized by extreme timidity. He looked down upon them because none of them seemed to him to be able to stand comparison with his mother. For him there was only one woman worthy of his love and admiration: his mother. With youthful fanaticism, he adopted all her views on art, and professed on everything the same ideas that she did.

As happens in the case of many parents, André's mother failed to take into account the fact that her son had ceased to be a child. She was still fondling him and smothering him with kisses at sixteen, exactly the way she did when he was six years old. Normally it is the children themselves that resist the excessive manifestations of affection from their mothers when they reach puberty, and force their less perceptive parents to come to the realization that they have left childhood behind. Not virile enough, André did nothing of the kind. Quite the contrary. He visibly took delight in his role of the cherished little boy, and without embarrassment took advantage of the situation to indulge his laziness. He experienced no embarrassment at the thought of living at his mother's expense, and had no desire whatever to make a living on his own.

André himself was unable to understand how one evening, when he was about sixteen, he became his mother's lover. She was about forty years old at the time. Mother and son both found themselves equally upset about what had "happened" to them and realized that it must never happen again. The psychologist to whom André was sent the very next day therefore had no difficulty in forbidding the repetition of incest; but he did find it necessary to allow plenty of time for bringing about a normalization of the relations between André and his mother on the emotional level. He had to prevent André from coming to despise his mother, and from holding her responsible for an act the young man was terribly ashamed of. He had to emphasize psychological extroversion therefore, and to suggest that André learn a trade and actively participate in the life of young people of his own age. In one sense, and from a strictly medical point of view, it was actually "good" for André to have experienced such a violent shock. If he had not, the chances are that his fixation on his mother would have been prolonged indefinitely and would have made him a complete social failure.

2. Harmful Effects of the Oedipus Fixation

Yet, in spite of everything, true incest (both psychological and physical at the same time, as observed in the cases of Dominique and André) is rare enough. If the Oedipus complex concerned only such exceptional cases as these, there would be no valid reason to devote an entire chapter to it in a book dealing with the psychoanalysis of love. To be sure, the Oedipus fixation implies incest, but it goes far beyond that.

In his *Introduction to Psychoanalysis,* Freud writes, "Even while he is still a child, the son commences to experience a special feeling of affection for his mother. He considers her his possession and sees in the father a sort of rival who disputes his possession of this good." Exactly the same situation would be said to prevail in the case of little girls, who would love the father and view the mother as a rival. Allowing for certain nuances of interpretation, every depth psychologist cannot but confirm this thesis of the founder of psychoanalysis in the light of his own experience. The "Oedipus" situation, although not as universal as Freudians assume, is widespread enough. If the Oedipus complex were only that, it would be difficult to understand the many vehement objections against it, not only on the part of laymen but equally on the part of the most eminent specialists.

As a matter of fact, however, Freudian "Oedipism" goes much further than that. For example, Freudians consider it experimentally established that this preference of the child for the parent of the opposite sex is always of a sexual nature. This is something which is altogether debatable. It is true that in a certain number of neurotic individuals the Oedipus attachment manifests itself in such an extreme form. But in the majority of even these cases, there is no reason to speak of incest except in a purely analogous sense. These facts do not authorize an affirmation of a scientific character, that is to say, one of universal application. Here as with all the other complexes and almost all other psychological facts, the margin that has to be left to the individual and the undetermined is infinitely greater than it is in the respective domains of the various natural sciences. In particular, it is erroneous, from a methodological standpoint, to presume as valid for all human beings facts observed exclusively among neurotics. This is true even if these facts are encountered in every neurotic individual—something which certainly is not the case. Roland Dalbiez, one of the most objective critics of Freudian doctrine, writes (in keeping with good scientific method), "The Oedipus complex must be proved and not assumed." [2]

It is understood here, therefore, that the Oedipus complex is not universal, and that where one encounters it, it is generally only by abusing metaphor that one can equate it with incest. It is nevertheless undeniable that the affective fixation on the parent of the opposite sex is often the main obstacle to a person's love life, and not only in the case of subjects who are extremely neurotic.

Germaine, thirty years of age, considered herself very unhappy in her marriage. Eight years before, she had married an engineer with a good position, whose mistress she had been previously. A short time after their marriage, she realized that almost everything about her husband was displeasing to her. Short and fat, he lacked a distinguished appearance. Besides, he was not sufficiently interested in "things of the spirit," all his energy apparently being mobilized in the service of his professional career. She complained that he did not show enough affection either for her or their children. She betrayed him regularly, in the hope (which she herself knew to be false) of finding elsewhere the fullness of affection that was missing in her married life. She took great care not to become attached too deeply to any of her lovers, and in order to avoid all risk of this kind, she changed them frequently.

What strikes the psychologist immediately is the fact

[2] *The Psychoanalytic Method and the Doctrine of Freud* (New York: Longmans, 1949), I, p. 9.

that Germaine chose her lovers from among men appreciably older than herself, while her husband was just about her own age. There was no doubt—and analysis confirmed the fact—that she passionately loved her father who had died several years before her marriage. Not only was he the example of a perfect man in her eyes, but she spoke of him with such devotion one would think him a demi-god. Germaine's parents had not understood each other very well. Her mother was not capable of keeping up with her husband, who was an eminent university professor. Germaine recalled that at the age of ten she was already the companion and (she thought) the confidant of her father. They went for horse-back rides and long walks together. He talked to her about his books and ideas, and introduced her to the art and music which he liked. She did the impossible to try to understand him, or at least to listen to him with admiration, even when the flow of words he rained on her went over her head. She took enormous pains to learn to play the piano so she would be in a position to accompany him when he played the violin.

The parents did not share the same room, and apparently they had no intimate sexual relations with each other. Germaine was not jealous of her mother. Instead, she experienced only disdain and pity for this woman, whom she judged unworthy of a man like her father. But when she became a young girl she put on terrible scenes of jealousy before her father each time she saw him paying attention to a woman, and all the more so when she might suspect her to be his mistress. It was on the occasion of one such jealous rage that, at seventeen, she gave herself to the first boy she had met—not out of love or desire, but to get revenge on her father. She experienced terrible remorse, aggravated by the fact that her father died of a heart attack several months later. Until she was psychoanalyzed, she remained convinced that she had killed him because of her misconduct.

Germaine and her father had had no incestuous relations at all. There had never been the least gesture, the slightest word, even the faintest thought between them that would not have met the strictest demands of morality. But we know that sexuality is only one of the integral components of human affectivity. The latter can exist very strongly without the other in certain circumstances. In Germaine's case there was such an affective fixation on the father that she became incapable of having any other love or living any life in which her father was not the center. Her unconscious caused her to marry a man who was completely different from her father because her natural psychological vitality tended, all the same, toward independence. By this very fact, however, the marriage became a sort of betrayal. She therefore had to punish herself by rejecting in her married life (always unconsciously) both sexual pleasure and spiritual joy. She was firmly persuaded that her father would never have approved of her marriage with a man so different from himself.

In the person of her older lovers, she obviously was looking for a substitute for her father. She naturally could not expect from any one of them a love as sublime and pure as she had received from her father. It was in order not to betray him that she took such jealous care not to become attached to anyone. The circumstances of her first sexual experience and those of her married life had taught her to despise her body. The gift of her heart, infinitely more than the gift of her body, would have seemed to her to constitute infidelity with regard to her father.

In the course of the resolution of her Oedipus fixation in psychotherapy, Germaine put an end to her extramarital sexual experiences without regret. She became capable of living on good terms with her husband. She did not cherish her father's memory less, but it was now no longer the memory of an idol, but of a man who had his faults as well as his good qualities.

3. A Myth Invented by Freud

In the case of Germaine, and in the majority of cases I have known which have involved an Oedipus fixation, there is absolutely no reason whatsoever to interpret matters in terms of a primitive impulse of the sexual instinct, which only moral and social tabus have caused to turn in the direction of persons outside the family. Quite the contrary. If Germaine's love for her father went beyond the bounds of a normal filial love with the result that she became unable to love any other man when she became a woman, the fault—in so far as one can speak of a fault in this case—lies in the peculiar circumstances of the love life of her father. Not finding in his wife the companion-disciple which he, like so many other intellectuals, felt the need of having, the professor became interested in his daughter to a much greater extent than was desirable for the normal affective maturing of a child. He prevented her from turning spontaneously in the direction of the outside world.

It is significant that the Oedipus fixation rarely develops in those whose parents live together in complete affective harmony. Frequently it is because parents unconsciously are looking to their son or daughter for a substitute for the love they have not found from each other that they make room for an Oedipus fixation in their children.

It is important to insist again on the fact that it is only in completely exceptional cases that even a strong Oedipus fixation leads to incestuous love in the literal sense of the term. In any event, even in cases where such a love really exists, it seems in no way to be the result of a primitive tendency of the sexual instinct. Quite the reverse is true. The sexual instinct normally tends in the direction of *the other*, that is to say, in the direction of persons with whom the subject can least identify himself. Only more or less serious psychological conflicts can cause this natural movement to be replaced by narcissism. For incestuous love is largely narcissistic, just as the Oedipus fixation itself is narcissistic, as we had occasion to observe in the case of Germaine.

Freud tried hard to prove that the Oedipus complex (in the sense of an incestuous love) is primitive and universal, and in addition that it explains practically every kind of psychological conflict. Since experience could not furnish proof of such statements, Freud invented the myth of a kind of Oedipal original sin.

Originally, he recounts, humanity lived in a gregarious state. No one possessed an individual consciousness. The strongest males appropriated all the females to themselves, and this left the young and those who were less strong in the position of being unable to satisfy their sexual needs except in a clandestine manner. One day, one of the

young males, in order to possess one of the females—
who happened to be his own mother—killed her partner
(who was his own father). This was the "historical"
origin of the complex described in the Oedipus legend.
The young parricide felt himself guilty of a terrible crime.
Thereafter, in some mysterious hereditary way, this feeling
of guilt becomes implanted in the unconscious of all
human beings. This is the source of our moral laws, and
particularly of all sexual prohibitions and tabus. Since the
sexual impulse was the cause of so great a crime, man
reasons unconsciously that it must be an accursed thing
by nature. The majority of neurotics exhaust their
energy with this same Oedipus guilt complex. Incestuous
love is also the heritage of the ancient passion of a son
for his mother.

Freud is not the only one of the masters of depth
psychology to try to find psychological doctrines in myths
and legends. It is well known how important a place
mythology occupies in Jungian psychology. The perspec-
tives in which myths and legends are placed by Freud
and by Jung, however, are radically different from each
other. For Jung studied the mythological traditions of
primitive peoples in a personal and profound way, while
Freud obtained his information at second hand. He even
went so far as to fabricate a myth out of whole cloth—
like the one described above—in order to obtain a
"proof" for a theory which seemed necessary to the
coherence of his system. On the other hand, Jung based
several of his most celebrated theories—for example,
those relating to the collective unconscious and the
archetypes—on myths which actually belong to the cultur-
al deposit of several peoples. The man the Freudians
accuse of dabbling in "mysticism" behaved like a true
man of science. Unfortunately the same cannot always be
said of Freud.

In fact, as seductive as the Freudian explanation of the
Oedipus and the guilt complex may appear to certain
minds, its grave defect is that it is not supported by any
observable facts, but is simply the product of Freud's
imagination. Rejecting the hypothesis of certain sociolo-
gists of the nineteenth century, not a single student of
ethnology or a serious historian today maintains the
thesis that the primitive condition of human beings was a

gregarious one. The individual consciousness undoubtedly exists even among the most primitive people even though, by comparison with the consciousness of civilized men, it is manifested in a very rudimentary form. But, in particular, the incest of the young man-animal, and the related murder of the father, cannot be grounded on any mythological indications. One may or may not admire the poetic invention of Freud, but it is absolutely impossible to derive from it the slightest teaching on the level of depth psychology. The Oedipus complex operates effectively in the psychism of a certain number of persons, but as we said before (in agreement with Dalbiez), it must be established in each particular case and never simply be assumed.

4. Incestuous Love between Brothers and Sisters

Many novelists have more or less skilfully handled the theme of the brother and sister who have been separated from infancy and do not know each other, and who later meet and fall hopelessly in love. The discovery of their common parentage provides occasion for a dramatic dénouement more or less similar to that which developed out of the love of Jocasta and Oedipus. This literary theme presupposes a strong erotic attraction between brothers and sisters, an attraction which only moral constraints prevent from normally manifesting itself.

The psychologist has no reason to deny a priori the existence of such an attraction. In the first place, the known cases of incestuous love between brothers and sisters are numerous enough, and here again we are not at all referring to fortuitous sexual relations that occur because of unfavorable social conditions. Besides, as we mentioned before, love tends spontaneously in the direction of a person who is most like ourselves yet also different. It is true that there are children born of the same parents who are very unlike one another, both physically and psychologically. But it is not difficult to discover also innumerable, deep, hidden affinities between them. It is certain that education and morals play a great role in explaining the fact that brothers and sisters only rarely take one another for the subject of their eroticism.

Sexual play between brothers and sisters in early childhood is relatively widespread. It would be wrong, however, to draw from this an argument in support of the notion of incestuous love. It is simply a matter of being able to satisfy curiosity more easily between themselves than with strangers. Several years before puberty, however, the relations between brothers and sisters generally become very modest—more modest than their relations with strangers.

Estelle, who was eleven years old, made a shameful reputation for herself because of her excessive sexual curiosity. Not only did she "touch herself," but she practiced exhibitionism and mutual touches with boys from her school or ones who lived in her immediate neighborhood. With her brothers, however, she displayed such extreme modesty that she took special care to make sure that they never saw her undressed. She took many precautions, dressing or changing into a bathing suit on the beach, for example. She vaguely remembered having engaged in certain habitual sexual play with her brothers when she was about six or seven, but these were memories of a painful and shameful nature, and she repressed them.

When the love between brothers and sisters becomes clearly erotic, it is my observation that it almost always begins in a fortuitous way.

Arlette was eighteen years old when she was entrusted to the care of a psychologist because of her scholastic difficulties. It appeared that for the past four years she had been having sexual relations with her brother, who was a year older than she. She did not recall any sexual behavior during their childhood, and she herself experienced only very little curiosity about "things like that." She and her brother were "good friends"; they liked each other very much although they had their squabbles, but they never experienced any special feelings of tenderness for each other. They never kissed each other, even on the cheek. When the parents might go out of an evening, Arlette was afraid to remain alone in her room. Sometimes, unable to overcome her fear, she asked her brother to come to sleep in her bed until the parents returned or she fell asleep. It was under these circumstances that, about the age of fourteen, she noticed an erection on her "little brother." Both of them were equally ignorant about sexual matters. "In a spirit of playfulness," she said, they made love several days later under the same circumstances without really understanding what was happening to them. Having made a habit of it, they continued. The first few times, Arlette had hardly any consciousness of doing anything wrong. To be sure, the parents must not ever learn about it, but there are so many things one cannot tell one's parents! It was not until she was about sixteen, when she had become fully a young lady and was beginning to be courted by young men, that she fully realized the "monstrousness" of her fault.

Smitten by remorse and afraid to confide in anyone, Arlette became extremely nervous and began to do poorly at school. Toward her brother she no longer experienced love, but hate. She also assured me (and there is no reason not to believe her) that she never loved him "the way a girl loves a boy." She is convinced that feelings never played the slightest role in the sexual desire that united them. I am not in a position to know whether the same situation prevailed in the case of her brother.

Arlette resolved many times not to do it again with her brother. When her parents went out in the evening, she barricaded the door to her room with chairs and a table. But when her brother nevertheless succeeded in getting into her room, she rarely had the strength—"moral strength," she explained—to resist him. Worse yet, it happened that after having barricaded herself, she sometimes took the initiative herself to go to her brother. In the hope of being freed from the obsession that drove her toward her brother, she several times gave herself to some of her male friends. She found no pleasure in it, however, and with a renewed impulse, began again with her brother, reluctantly, and considering herself vile. Analysis revealed that sexual pleasure in her case was tied up strictly with her feeling of guilt and anxiety. It would be necessary to rid her of this feeling before she would be able to find herself delivered from her fatal passion.

The relations between Arlette and her brother were incestuous even if it could be established that in the case of neither one of them was there any question of real love. Nothing gives us the right to conclude from this, however, that it is a matter of a primitive incestuous inclination which is innate. On the contrary. There is every reason to believe that if either of these two children had been exposed to the same kind of intimate situation with any other boy or girl, things would have turned out the same way. And if the parents had paid more attention to their little girl's fears when they were away, very probably these two children would never have experienced any incestuous attraction for each other. Instead of concluding from the known facts about fraternal incest to the universality or quasi-universality of an incestuous drive, one is actually amazed that similar cases are not much more numerous than one finds when he takes into account how easily the opportunity is afforded.

The only conclusion that can be drawn from the cases we have observed is that *in itself* the sexual instinct has no radical aversion to incest. Education and moral principles, anchored deeply in the unconscious, are undoubtedly the principle reasons why incestuous deviations of the *libido* are relatively rare. In any case, it is incorrect to speak of an inclination of an incestuous nature in normal persons. It is a question of perversion, of emotional illness, except when it is a matter of a tragic accident, as in several of the cases presented here.

To prevent incestuous relations like those between Arlette and her brother from establishing themselves, it is clearly not enough simply to increase one's vigilance. There will always be ways of eluding vigilance. The parents of these two children made a mistake, of course, in allowing them to sleep together in their absence, when the children were on the threshold of adolescence. But they made an even greater mistake by far in not having given their attention to the progressive affective and sexual education of their children.

CHAPTER FIVE

THE "PARAPHILIAE"

CERTAIN KINDS of love are considered normal within the confines of a given civilization, or almost universally; other kinds are looked upon as abnormal and unnatural. Freudian psychoanalysis raises its voice in indignation against the claim that such a distinction implies a value judgment. Speaking of infantile sexuality, Freud declares that the child is a "polymorphous pervert." He was evidently not unaware of how shocking such a "definition" would seem to public opinion, accustomed as it is to view the child as a "little angel."

Coming from the pen of the founder of psychoanalysis, however, the word "pervert" possesses none of the pejorative signification attached to it in ordinary language. This is simply Freud's way of saying that, so far as its object and its form of expression are concerned, the sexual instinct possesses no particular determination in the beginning, except to tend of itself to its own satisfaction. It would be only accidentally (and generally under the social influence of education) that the instinct would become fixed on a certain particular object to the exclusion of all others. Therefore, Freud might just as well have used the expression "normal polymorph" in place of "polymorphous pervert," except that his desire to shock made him prefer the latter designation.

Neither the observations nor the speculations of the Freudians are sufficient to support the conclusion that the sexual instinct in its original state is undifferentiated with regard to its object and its goal. Quite the contrary. Everything points to the fact that it is not by accident that the sexual instinct in a man tends in the direction of a woman, and in a woman tends in the direction of a man. Nor is it by chance that it generally makes use of just those parts of the body known as the *sexual organs*

91

to procure its satisfaction. To use the language of Freud, neither the choice of this "object" nor the choice of this "goal" requires explanation any more than there is a need to explain why man uses his mouth in order to eat and his anus in order to defecate.

It is nevertheless undeniable that more often than is commonly supposed the sexual instinct is given a goal and an object that is different from the normal. Since we are interested in sexuality as an integral part of love, we shall consider its deviations to the extent that they have an effect upon the love life of human beings.

I did not want to title this chapter "Perverted Forms of Love" because the word "perverted" commonly implies a judgment (if not a condemnation) of a moral character. The psychologist realizes that the deviations of affective energy in question very often hardly involve the moral responsibility of the subject at all. Instead, they represent psychic illnesses of a more or less serious nature. I have therefore preferred to adopt the more neutral term of "paraphilia" to signify a love that is a-natural or a love that runs parallel to the normal.

1. *Narcissism*

According to the legend, a handsome youth named Narcissus saw his own reflection in water. He found it so attractive that he fell passionately in love with it. No other person being of interest to him any longer, he himself became the sole, fascinating object of his own love. One day, stretching down his arms to embrace his double, he fell into the water and was drowned.

Since Freud, psychologists have made use of the term, narcissism, to describe those whose *libido,* or power to love, makes their own ego the object of their love, instead of reaching out in the direction of another person. This is the case with many who are either neurotic or psychotic. They are preoccupied exclusively with themselves and believe themselves to be superior to everyone else, or at least to be the object of general interest. Convinced that everyone is concerned about them, sometimes for good but more often for ill, they readily become the victims of a persecution mania. The majority of paranoiacs are narcissists.

In conformity with the general principles of his theory of sexuality, Freud sees in narcissism a first phase of love which all human beings go through. Love for another person occurs only at a much later stage. Admitting no specific difference whatsoever between the oral pleasure the infant derives from sucking at the breast, the anal pleasure he experiences in defecating, and sexual pleasure, the founder of psychoanalysis thought that "many sexual tendencies achieve in the beginning a satisfaction which we call *auto-erotic,* that is to say, a satisfaction whose source is the subject's own body, and that it is the tendency toward auto-eroticism which explains the tardiness with which sexuality adapts itself to the reality-principle inculcated by education. Thus it is that auto-eroticism is the sexual activity of the narcissistic phase of the *libido's* fixation." [1]

Elsewhere I have elaborated the compelling reasons which lead me to reject the Freudian general theory of sexuality.[2] Its greatest weakness lies in the fact that instead of being founded upon experience it interprets experience in the light of the exigencies of its own doctrinal postulates. Freudianism is also in error when it tries to study human sexuality without taking into account the intrinsic relationship which unites it to love: the psychic element in eroticism.

Both the sexual impulse and the power to love exist in each individual at first only in a purely potential state. For its awakening, love presupposes the duality of a subject and an object, even if this is perceived only very dimly in consciousness at the very first stage. Normally it is a person of the opposite sex which the *libido* chooses as its object. It is as a result of the intervention of certain other factors—sometimes external but more often internal to the subject, and of an unconscious nature—that these impulses are susceptible of being led in a devious direction away from their normal path. The *libido* can then become fixed on the very person of the loving subject himself, or can take as its object a person of the same sex. In that event, it becomes necessary to speak of narcissism and auto-eroticism.

Narcissism is not necessarily the equivalent of egoism.

---

[1] *Introduction to Psychoanalysis.*
[2] Cf. my *Clartés et ténèbres de l'âme.*

An individual can be a complete egoist and still love another person. He loves the other person solely for himself. He seeks in love only his own emotional or sensual satisfaction. He considers himself indispensable for the other person without realizing what he himself is deriving from their relationship. This is clearly a case of narcissism. Then there are persons who are not egoists and who are nevertheless narcissists. Such persons are indifferent to any erotic or sexual object other than themselves.

It is wrong to consider masturbation in adolescents as a sign of narcissistic deviation. The awakening of their sexual and emotional impulses is in the direction of another person. It is because the other person (particularly if it is the one they are in love with) is pictured as inaccessible that, consciously or not, a substitute is sought in "solitary pleasure." In my observation, even the interest which many adolescents manifest in their own bodies is not at all auto-erotic in its origin.

Masturbation is a sign of narcissism only if it carries over into adulthood. The adolescent procures his pleasure as a substitute for the pleasure he imaginatively would prefer to find with another. The adult who masturbates habitually, however, is looking to avoid any real emotional contact with another person. Some of them regularly flee every opportunity for such contact and encase themselves behind a wall of bitter isolation. Others gladly enter into social relationships with other people. They would suffer from the lack of them. They fail to appreciate, however, that it is they themselves who are the obstacle which prevents any relationship from becoming a deep one.

Maurice, a history student, twenty-four years of age, was not antisocial in any way. He enjoyed the company of his friends. He had a marked preference for those of them who were women. But he did not succeed in experiencing the smallest degree of affection or the slightest degree of sexual desire for any of them. His relationship with women remained strictly on an esthetic and intellectual level, exactly like his relationship with men. He obtained sexual pleasure by himself, without so much as an image or a thought that might relate to another person. He was completely insensitive to the naked body of a handsome man or a beautiful woman. The only thing that excited him in an erotic way was the contemplation of his own body. While he masturbated, his mind dwelt fondly on himself. His erotic narcissism was complete, therefore, but without his being an egoist. He was spontaneously altruistic enough in his habitual behavior with others.

Absolute narcissism is relatively rare. It is encountered only among neurotics. But the love life of a great many men and women is poisoned by what can be called a relative narcissism. These individuals love another person, sexually and emotionally, but their love does not at all succeed in getting them out of their egocentricity. Their love is in no way a self-giving type of love. Its character is exclusively possessive. They make demands but they refuse to give, and especially they refuse to give themselves. They are not generally considered to be neurotic. Their narcissism can be explained in terms of residues of an affective infantilism which has not as yet been overcome. The result is painful psychological conflicts for the subject himself and much suffering for the person he loves.

After fifteen years of marriage, Charlotte said that she still loved her husband. It was clear, however, that what she called love was a strange mixture of fear and resentment. It was enough for her husband to be a little late for her to imagine him the victim of an accident at work or on the way home. She cried, trembled, prayed to all the saints in heaven. No sooner had he crossed the threshold of the house, however, when far from going into transports of joy, she heaped reproaches upon him, holding him responsible for her torment of a little while ago. Unlike the normal person in love whose dominant desire is "to please," Charlotte thought only of herself in a neurotic way. When she imagined her husband the victim of an accident, it was not at all about his suffering that she was thinking, but only of herself: "What would become of me if I were left alone?" When he was sick, she took care of him with a devotion worthy of admiration. But as soon as he began to get well and she no longer had any need to take care of him, she was annoyed at seeing him lying in bed, doing nothing, while she had to "wear herself out." Although her husband

was more educated than she, she rarely allowed him to
express his thoughts and opinions or to talk about things
that interested him: so great was her conviction that
anything foreign to her own ideas and interests could not
have any value. Her narcissism was not least evident in
the very way she obtained her sexual pleasure. Her partner served simply as an instrument to procure it for her.
Even from her children she required veneration and adoration. She expected them to give her pleasure.

To prevent this woman from making herself unhappy
(for she was unhappy in the midst of all these demands),
from making those she loved unhappy, and from finally
destroying her home, it was necessary to teach her how
to love in an outgoing way. It was a question of eliminating her affective infantilism, of which the narcissism was
only the effect.

2. Homosexuality

Homosexual love-relationships are certainly much more
frequent than it is commonly believed. I am not speaking
here of homosexual relations between men and between
women who are in prisons or in other places where
relations with representatives of the other sex are rendered physically impossible. In the majority of cases, affectivity is hardly involved at all in such relationships.
Their sole purpose seems to be the "physical" satisfaction
of the sexual instinct. The affectivity of these individuals
is almost completely normal, and they resume heterosexual
relations as soon as the doors of the prison open up to
let them out.

Before getting into the heart of the subject, it would be
appropriate to ask ourselves, however, whether or not we
are right in considering heterosexuality the only normal
kind of sexuality, and consequently homosexuality as
abnormal and unnatural. Many homosexuals, pointing to
the authority of psychoanalysis, vigorously contest the
validity of such a distinction between normal and abnormal sexuality According to Freud the sexual instinct has
no precise object "by nature," as we have already seen,
and tends only to its own satisfaction. It is only by
chance or under the influence of external constraint that
the instinct becomes fixed in the direction of one type of

object rather than some other. As a matter of fact, if the majority of men practice heterosexuality, it is due solely to social pressure. Society is interested in putting sexuality at the service of reproduction; it forbids by its moral codes and its laws any expressions of sexuality which go in a direction contrary to this goal.

Because I believe the idea of the determination of each instinct by its specific object to be scientifically incontestable, it is impossible for me to agree with the Freudian theory of the instincts. Instincts are capable of being turned in the direction of a "foreign" object only by accident. As soon as it is awakened, the sexual instinct normally tends in the direction of a person of the opposite sex. It often enough happens, however, that this spontaneous movement is inhibited by internal and external causes.

Homosexual love is certainly more frequently encountered in civilizations and environments in which a strict separation of the two sexes is practiced among adolescents. This is the case in Islamic countries, for example, first because of the physical segregation of the sexes, but also because of the way of life for women in those countries, which renders them almost completely unable to have any genuine existential communication. It is common there to see two young men, or even two mature men, walking hand in hand as lovers, whispering tender secrets into each other's ear. It is not at all a proven fact, however, that in every case this homosexual love implies a deviation of a properly genital character. As for Moslem women, it is equally true that very often they too look among themselves for the affective satisfactions which custom prevents them from obtaining from men.

In many boarding schools, the first object of the flame of love is almost always a fellow student or an admired teacher. Homosexual relations of a physical nature, however, are certainly infinitely less frequent than certain novelists would have us believe. In the majority of cases, homosexual love is only a temporary affair. Often all it takes is vacation-time for the adolescent to become enamored of a cousin or, as a result of a mechanism well known to psychologists, of the sister of his favorite comrade. This is enough of itself to establish the ungenuine character of homosexual love. When a case of a true homosexual fixation is encountered, it is generally because certain external conditions of life have come to be engrafted onto a psychologically predisposed soil.

Fernand, a thirty-five-year-old school teacher, was desperate because of his inability to experience love for women. He would have liked so much to have established a home and to have had a "normal life." Twice he became engaged on the advice of friends who told him that "love would come later." But each time his "instinctive" aversion for any kind of intimacy with the woman displayed itself very strongly. Not only did he not experience any sexual attraction for either of his fiancées, but it repelled him to have to kiss either of them or take either of them into his arms. The idea of soon having to share his bed made him nauseous. It was impossible for him not to experience a woman as a creature who was impure.

Fernand himself attributed his inability to love women to the "bad habits" contracted at the normal school which he began to attend at the age of sixteen. But he recalled that even before that he had been "madly in love" with one of his teachers. He had followed him as a shadow, had been desperately jealous of his feminine companions, and had written him some passionate love letters. But the teacher, although he was very kind to Fernand, very obviously preferred female loves. At the normal school, Fernand suddenly fell in love with a fellow student who was a year older than himself. It was with him that he experienced his initiation into homosexual practices. He had not become, as he said, a common pederast. He never entertained the idea or even experienced the temptation, for example, to seduce one of his pupils. But for almost twenty years, he had been experiencing feelings of love, living in a place in which there were only men. Sometimes he would have sexual relations, particularly if it was a question of someone who already had been initiated to "the thing"; but very often his love remained platonic. In either case, he experienced shame at being abnormal, and he bore a terrible resentment toward his first seducer at the normal school.

In the course of psychological treatment, it began to appear that the responsibility of the "seducer" was appreciably less than Fernand himself believed, or at least that his action would not have had such profound effects if the soil had not been well prepared. As a child Fernand had been very attached to his mother. Frustrated and unhappy in her married life, she showered all her pent-up affection on her son. At the age of twelve he was still sleeping in his mother's bed. They exchanged confidences "the way girls do," and he conducted himself in other respects like a girl, to his mother's great pleasure. His inability to love women stemmed initially from the unconscious identification of all women with his mother. It would have seemed to him to be betraying her. In addition to this, he identified himself with his mother and, like her, he could love only men. However, Fernand was not effeminate in appearance.

In almost every case of homosexual deviation I have been able to observe, fixation on the mother seems to have played the decisive role. Sometimes the mother has brought up her son as a girl; sometimes she has subjected him to her excessive expressions of love, and sometimes— as in the case of Fernand—there has been a combination of these two equally mistaken lines of conduct. The result is almost always the same in practice. In the one case, the unconscious having identified all women with the mother, it is the fear of incest (perhaps of an unconsciously desired incest, if one is to believe Freud) which renders heterosexual love impossible. In the other case, it is self-identification with the mother who does not love women (but often hates them because one of them has deprived her of her husband's love) which prevents a man from being in a position to love women.

In certain cases homosexual deviation may be the consequence of the Oedipus complex in reverse. Dalbiez relates a typical case which was treated by Doctor Breuer. Girolamo, a child of frail health in a large peasant family, had received almost no attention from his mother because she was too busy to bother with him. Instead, it was the father who took charge of him, especially in the winter time when he had a great deal of spare time. "About the age of seven, sleeping with his father, Girolamo accidentally touched his father's penis. It gave him an erection. . . . The attention he had received from his father instead of from his mother—which would have been the normal case—had determined his first orientation in the direction of a man. His physical weakness and the scornful allusions to his lack of ability inspired a fear of masculinity in him. So disposed, it was only natural that he should identify with his sister." Unconsciously fearful of incest because of this identification with his sister, Girolamo became incapable of loving a woman, no matter who she was. As for his attraction to men, that would seem to be the result both of his great attachment to his father and of his identification with his sister. Like her, he loved men.

3. Lesbianism

Contrary to current opinion, homosexual love seems to be even more frequent among women than among men, although the fixation among men is generally much less exclusive in character. The first flame of an adolescent girl is almost always a woman teacher or a girl friend who is considerably older than herself. This is due largely to the fear of men which education and custom instills in the young girl at a very early age. A man is the big danger for them. Every man is made to appear as virtually a seducer. If a girl is on friendly terms with a man, she risks compromising her reputation. Girls who have had a few furtive experiences of an intimate nature with young men at a party know that they are not easily contented with the little attentions and the tender caresses that affect a girl. Young men are inclined to interpret the fact that their caresses were welcomed as an encouragement to "go further." Besides, almost all girls think about marriage. They are aware of the fact that these same young men who show themselves so eager to deprive them of their virginity, do not want to marry a girl who is not a virgin. They are also familiar with the sorry plight of unwed mothers in society. Under such conditions, it is not at all astonishing that only the unwary experience no fear at all of being in the company of men.

Endowed with a more refined sensibility and with greater emotionality, the young girl experiences the need to love and to be loved much more intensely than the young man. Very naturally, therefore, her impulse is directed to a "friend of her heart." No one sees anything wrong in what two young girls do together. It seems perfectly natural for them to walk arm in arm, to kiss each other frequently, and to exchange tender confidences in conversation and letters. It is apparently all quite "platonic." This is partially true, although the depth psychologist almost always discovers that the caresses and the kisses create an emotional experience in the two girls which he knows is erotic but which they themselves consider "purely affectionate."

The lesbian loves of adolescent girls do not represent a true homosexual fixation in the majority of cases. It is a question of substitute or displaced love. As soon as the circumstances are propitious, the young girl will not hesitate to prefer the attentions of a man to that of her best girl friend. This is true even when the relations between the two friends have been explicitly erotic. The transition from lesbian love of a platonic kind to lesbian love of an erotic character is generally brought about by the influence of an older woman who initiates it.

At sixteen, Susanne was madly in love with one of her professors, who was twenty-seven. When the latter kissed her on the cheek one day, to show her appreciation for a kindness, she fluttered with joy and pleasure. Each time the opportunity presented itself, she sought out her company and often found a way to bring about a situation that called for caresses and kisses between them. During vacation, the professor invited Susanne to go camping with her. The young girl's parents naturally saw no reason to object. In the tent, they became lovers in an explicit way. It lasted for about two weeks. At the end of the vacation period, a complete separation took place when the professor was given an appointment in another city.

I do not know whether or not Susanne's professor had been a true, experienced lesbian. Two years later, Susanne fell in love with one of her girl friends while she was a student living at the university. She soon began to initiate her to the pleasures of Lesbos. She eventually became a professor herself. Almost every year, she fell in love with one of her pupils whom she managed to get to desire and accept her caresses. She became an extremely adept seductress. "Adept" is hardly the proper word. Each time, as a matter of fact, Susanne was sincerely convinced that this time it was the "great love" of her life.

It is important to realize that Susanne was in no way

masculine in her manner. Very much the feminine co-
quette, she dressed stylishly. She felt no repugnance
whatever for men. In fact, she actively desired to be loved
by a man, hoping such a love would free her from her
"vice." She would have preferred to be married. Only,
she maintained, she did not know how to attract men.
Her position as a professor in a girls' school provided her
with little opportunity to meet men. One day, sadly
disappointed once again by the "desertion" of her friend,
who had come to prefer "some man or other," Susanne
decided to take her problems to a psychotherapist.

It appears that as a child Susanne had been very
attached to her father, whom she also feared very much.
A severe man, he often punished her for the slightest
infraction of family discipline. At a very young age, she
realized that her mother was unhappy in her marriage.
Her mother often complained to her friends, in the presence of her little daughter, of the brutality and lack of
understanding of men for their wives. Little Susanne felt
pity for married women, who were at the mercy of the
whims of tyrant-husbands. When she was seven years
old, Susanne and a boy-cousin of her own age were
caught in the act of observing the different way in which
"boys and girls are made." She was given a spanking.
From puberty on, her mother continually "dinned into
her ears" warnings to be on her guard against men.
From that time on, she sought them at the same time
that she fled from them. When at sixteen she experienced
the pleasures of love for the first time in the arms of her
professor friend, she imagined she was in the arms of a
man. Later, when she herself had become a seductress
and an initiator of young girls into "those pleasures," she
always managed not to have to assume only the masculine
role. She also wanted to be desired and possessed like a
woman.

From all the evidence, it would be yielding to the spirit
of systematization to consider Susanne and others like her
as "born" lesbians. There is certainly no problem of genes
or of hormones in such cases. It seems to me that it
would be more correct to have recourse to psychological
determinism as an explanation for such behavior. In the
case of Susanne, the events in her childhood and her
education as an adolescent undoubtedly had rendered

more numerous and more formidable the obstacles to the natural flight of their first amorous impulses toward a man which almost all young girls encounter in our civilization. If she had not met with the woman who initiated her, the chances are that she would have become involved with heterosexual love of a more or less satisfactory nature. It is undeniable, of course, that even the imperfect pleasure derived from lesbian love-relationships makes it difficult for a woman to overcome her unconscious prohibitions against love for a man, hard as she may try. A few months of therapy were enough to enable Susanne to normalize her amorous tendencies.

It is not only young girls, inexperienced in the ways of heterosexual love, who seek the pleasures of Sappho. Of those who give themselves over to them deliberately and in a sexual way, it seems that the greater number is to be found among married women. It is evidently a question of women who have been disappointed emotionally or sexually in their married life. Certain intellectual types in particular resent having to assume the subordinate position of the "second sex" which custom imposes on the wife. They married with the hope of establishing a person to person relationship of a stable nature. Little by little, they discover that neither the customs of our present society, nor the superiority complex with which they are afflicted with regard to their husband, favors such an interpersonal communion. Such a woman looks for understanding first, then for affection, and finally for pleasure from another woman who is herself often the victim of masculine ostracism. Some of them admit that this pleasure has not the same value for them as the pleasure they find in the company of men, but they give themselves over to it because in that way they experience a feeling of getting revenge on men and of proving to themselves that they are in the position to do without them.

The cause of matrimonial disillusionment and subsequent homosexuality in the case of certain women is their persistent narcissism. "Between man and woman," writes Simone de Beauvoir, "love is an act; each torn from self becomes other: what fills the woman in love with wonder is that the languorous passivity of her flesh should be reflected in the male's impetuosity; the narcissistic woman, however, recognizes her enticements but dimly in the man's erected flesh. Between women love is contemplative; caresses are intended less to gain possession of the other than gradually to re-create the self through her; separateness is abolished, there is no struggle, no victory, no defeat; in exact reciprocity each is at once subject and object, sovereign and slave; duality becomes mutuality. ... The lover takes delight in being sure of caressing a body the secrets of which she knows, and whose preferences her own body indicates to her." [3] Because she is incapable of getting outside herself, of communicating with someone who is truly an *other*, the narcissist "naturally" prefers the love of another woman to the love of a man.

Before marrying at the age of eighteen, Marie Louise had had no affective experience of either a homosexual or a heterosexual nature. She was an only child, and her mother wanted her to be with her always. Even her education was received through correspondence courses. Marie Louise therefore had not even had a "best girl friend." She experienced her defloration on the wedding night as a painful duty since her husband seems not to have been aware of the difference between the sensibility of a young virgin and that of a prostitute. During eight years of married life, she very rarely experienced any physical pleasure in the arms of her husband. She gradually developed into an indolent woman, bereft of vitality and enthusiasm. The trauma of her wedding night had the effect of implanting in her unconscious a tenacious rancor toward her husband and, by a process of identification (although to a lesser degree), toward men in general. She admitted it was largely her own fault that little by little her husband came to ignore her completely, since she "had been unable to prevent herself from rendering her company disagreeable to him," and she evidently had refused absolutely to experience any deep communion with him.

In the great emotional solitude from which she was suffering, Marie Louise undoubtedly could have taken a lover. She knew she was pretty and desirable, and masculine advances to her were not wanting. It was not that moral scruples prevented her. She thought that since her husband had not made her happy, she owed him no

[3] *The Second Sex* (New York: Knopf, 1953), pp. 416-417.

fidelity save the safeguarding of his "honor," something which it seemed to her could easily be taken care of. But she thought that taking a lover would involve too many complications "for the little satisfaction one could hope to derive from it." One would have to arrange for the secret rendezvous, be subjected to the humiliation of the looks of the hotel doormen, experience restlessness at having to return to a life of outward conformity to the rules of married life, and so on. Her marital disillusionment had made her too passive to become involved in such "complications."

She became the intimate friend of another young woman, hardly happier in her homelife than Marie Louise was in hers. Little by little, they discovered that not only could they console each other, but that they were able to experience in each other's arms a pleasure that was at least as satisfying as what they were receiving from their husbands. Since no one would have suspected them of being "two women of the world" who might engage in such things, they had all the freedom in the world to come together as often as they wished.

It seems that with respect to strictly sexual pleasure, homosexual love relations are as satisfying as heterosexual relations in the case of both men and women. Certain individuals who have experimented with both declare that sometimes the former are less disappointing than the latter. Some women who are completely frigid with men succeed without difficulty in having an orgasm with another woman. I have known one man at least who, having practiced homosexual and heterosexual relations side by side, maintained that he obtained pleasure from the former of a kind that was appreciably more intense than what he derived from the latter. It should be pointed out, however, and psychotherapeutic experience bears this out, that a preference given to homosexual pleasure is not exclusively physical in its origin. In the realm of human sexuality (as we indicated before) it is impossible to divorce the physical pleasure from its psychological context.

If the reality of love is examined in all its complexity, comprising as it does both sexual and psychological elements, there can be no question but that homosexual love is objectively less satisfying than heterosexual love. Not only is there no procreation involved, but it is uncreative in every respect. It is not in a position to give rise to that sort of multiplication of forces and increment of energy which normally result from the realization of heterosexual love. In a spirit of bravado, reacting against the scorn or the pity of which they are the object, certain homosexuals maintain that they are perfectly adjusted to their inversion. They state that they do not want to exchange it for what society considers the only normal kind of love. Actually, however, almost all of them suffer at least unconsciously from their inability to love "normally."

4. Sado-Masochistic Loves

In one of his novels, Gogol speaks of a Russian peasant woman who upset all her neighbors by her tears and complaints. When the village housewives urged her to tell them what the trouble was, she replied, "Oh, I'm so unhappy. Ivan does not love me any more. Here it is a whole month now and he has not beaten me up."

To those who know love only in a theoretical way, this anecdote will undoubtedly seem incomprehensible. Love being by definition an existential communion, it must manifest itself only in the form of tender caresses and endearing exchanges. Love's idealists are surprised to learn that even lovers who are completely normal and not afflicted with any sort of paraphilia, bite each other when they kiss, embrace each other in such a way as to make it hurt, and on occasion even pinch each other or slap each other. Many women like to feel themselves crushed in an amorous embrace, just as many men find pleasure in crushing or squeezing too tightly. And, I repeat, these men and women are "normal."

The two partners express themselves in love with their whole being. In the masculine psyche, the desire to protect the loved one is perfectly normal, but so is the need to conquer and possess her. In the normal man, these two elements are so intertwined that they mutually compensate each other. It would be completely wrong to see any sadistic paraphilia here. The latter exists only when the desire for possession is the predominant element in a love relationship, when one loves solely in order to be able to crush and humiliate the object of one's love.

The sadist is always a weakling. Humiliated and exploited by society, disappointed in his ambitions, the weakling finds in love the unique opportunity to get revenge. He can assert his strength and his will to power over the woman who, for the moment, he has in his grasp. It is his turn now to be able to cause suffering, and without the slightest threat to himself. These same sadistic weaklings are also very hard and authoritarian with children, servants, or anyone considered their inferior. They like to torment animals. It is wrong to view sadism as a purely sexual perversion. There is no reason to consider as sexual the pleasure such men experience in causing pain. It is true, however, that these men (who in their ordinary life in society are simply slaves) can feel themselves "masters" no place better than in bed. The mediocre husband of a woman who occupies a high social position used to brag to his friends at a bar, "She can do her strutting before the public. But in bed, I am the one who is on top of her, who gets into her, and makes her cringe." Actually, he could experience intense pleasure in amorous embrace only by mistreating the one he loved, whose superiority humiliated him.

Is passivity, the desire not only to be protected but also dominated, part of the make-up of a woman's "nature"? Is it not rather, as Simone de Beauvoir (the new-style feminist) maintains, the simple result of the condition under which women have lived throughout history in a society built by men to serve their own needs? The resolution of this purely theoretical debate is of scarcely any interest to our present psychological purposes. We are not studying here the eternal feminine or the feminine essence, but woman in the concrete, woman in actual situations. Viewed from this angle, it has to be admitted that the majority of women not only accept the situation which is theirs in a love relationship, but consider it as perfectly normal. Some young women, mainly intellectuals, staunchly hold out for their independence and protest indignantly against the state of dependency to which love has reduced some of their friends.

All that has to happen, however, is for one of these "strong" women to fall in love. Spontaneously, she will lean against the shoulder of the man she loves in such a way as to find herself in the position of being the one to

be protected. Even when she is much superior, morally
and physically, the normal woman is completely disposed
to give to the man she loves at least the appearances of
superiority. To be sure, this is partly a question of charity
or sensitivity, since she knows that a man likes to feel
himself the stronger of the two. The only women who
refuse to make such concessions or diplomatic gestures
are women who are more or less neurotic, women in
whom the assertion of virility is too strong. It would be
absurd to detect a trace of masochism in either the
spontaneous or the deliberate submission of a woman to
the man she loves. As we shall presently see, true sado-
masochistic paraphilia is something completely different
from the respective behavior of the man and woman in
the ordinary love situation.

Roger, aged forty, and Adele, twenty-eight, both having contracted unsatisfactory marriages "of reason," met
and immediately fell in love with each other. Adele was a
good woman, and it was only after long and persistent
pleading that she gave in and became Roger's mistress.
The second time they were together on an intimate basis,
Roger pulled a little whip out of his pocket and gave her
body a few light strokes. She could not understand it at
all. She thought it a joke in poor taste on the part of the
man whom she knew was otherwise quite refined. But
she laughed it off. The next time, however, he took out
his whip and asked her to whip him with all her strength.
Little by little, Adele discovered to her surprise that her
lover not only wanted to be whipped by her, but also
insulted and humiliated in all sorts of ways. This was not
only the way in which he intensified his sexual pleasure;
it was also the condition for his emotional expression. He
could not believe in the love of a woman who would not
agree to assault him physically and torment him psychologically. Adele experienced no pleasure whatever from
such practices. She found them repugnant, and it did not
take her long before she completely separated from her
lover.

The heroine of *Fort Frédéric*, a novel by Françoise de
Ligneries, is an unmarried woman in a chateau in an
obscure corner of a French province. A dominating woman, very jealous of her independence, she takes as a
lover a poor criminal who is being chased by the police.

She hides him from them in the chateau. She makes a slave of the brute, demands that he obey her in every respect, beats him and humiliates him. After a while, both of them manifest a desire to free themselves from this singular sado-masochistic relationship, and they take the first steps in that direction. But at the end of the story, the refined mistress of the chateau and the man who has nothing in his favor but the brute strength of his body realize that they are indispensible to each other. She loves him because she can dominate and humiliate him, and he can no longer live without her female domination. The one is as much a sadist as the other is a masochist.

There are an equal number of sadists and masochists, as many who experience the need to make the one they love suffer as there are those who desire to suffer. There are as many women as there are men in each group. It is not rare that an individual finds out about his sadistic or masochistic tendencies only by chance. There are persons in whom both tendencies exist together. They want both to suffer themselves and at the same time to cause another to suffer.

For a long time I was of the opinion that cases of true sado-masochism were very rare. If I am to trust the testimony of a "specialist" in this matter, it seems that I was very much mistaken. Apparently, there are a fairly large number of celebrated persons in the world of literature and the arts who consciously indulge in this type of love, not to mention the number of "obscure" amateurs.

What explanation of sadism and masochism is the depth psychologist in a position to give? The two cases I have observed personally are the one of Roger which I mentioned before, and another of a woman who in terms of her social origins sufficiently resembles the heroine of Françoise de Ligneries' novel.

As a small boy, and up until the time he was eleven years old, Roger had often been beaten on his buttocks with a stick by his nurse, whom he loved very much. He did not recall whether it was before or after he had reached the age of seven that this nurse, having whipped him much harder than she ever did before, took him in her arms to comfort him and "nicely" caressed him in the area of his sexual organs. He experienced a very keen pleasure from it, and probably also an erection. From then on, every time he was whipped on his bare bottom he experienced an erection. When he was thirteen, Roger asked one of his playmates to whip him on the buttocks. When his request was complied with, he experienced his first ejaculation. Around the age of twenty, he completely discontinued such practices. He thought he had even forgotten about the pleasure he used to get in this way. When he made his first attempts to have sexual relations, he appeared to be impotent. One day a prostitute, who was offended, struck him. He immediately experienced a lively pleasure, and recovered "all his powers." Ever since, whether it was a question of either physical or emotional love, it was absolutely necessary for him to experience it in a masochistic situation. Even a woman to whom he was most passionately attracted would lose all her attraction for him if she refused to beat and torment him. Occasionally, he found an intense psychological satisfaction in the lonely pangs of unrequited love. It was necessary for Roger to spend a long time in psychotherapy in order to have the idea of love and the idea of suffering disassociated in his unconscious.

Madame de M. had seen very little of her fiancé. Her marriage had been "arranged" for her, as is still the custom in a certain type of provincial good society. Totally ignorant about sexual matters, she dutifully abandoned herself to her husband, quickly became very attached to him and cherished him dearly. About two years after their honeymoon, she came home unexpectedly one day and surprised her husband in bed with his secretary. The shock was so great that she fainted and remained seriously ill for several weeks. "In some mysterious way," she then contracted pulmonary tuberculosis and had to go to a sanatorium for a long rest-cure. All the evidence points to the fact that she sought refuge in sickness in order to avoid the sight of her unfaithful husband.

Toward the end of her stay in the sanatorium, Madame de M. became the object of the attentions of a certain doctor. She found him pleasing, but for some reason completely incomprehensible to herself, she felt the need to make her admirer suffer in a thousand different little ways. She would give herself to him only after he begged on his knees and kissed her feet. Several times during an amorous embrace she slapped him very hard.

When she returned to her home, Madame de M. decided that since her resentment had not subsided, she could not have any contact with her husband, except what was expected out of strict politeness. She inflicted the same kind of bodily punishment on her lovers as she had on the doctor at the sanatorium, but it was more important to her to humiliate them. She treated them like slaves, and imposed tasks on them that lowered them in her own eyes. Although she never wanted for men to lend themselves with pleasure to her sadistic demands, at the same time, her evil joy and her disdain for the masculine sex in general increased. In order to rid Madame de M. of her sadistic tendencies, it would undoubtedly be necessary for her to experience a genuine reconciliation with her husband.

CHAPTER SIX

FRUSTRATED LOVE

IT IS possible for an individual to substitute one form of love for another. It is not possible, however, for a human being to achieve complete fulfillment without some kind of love. In a more or less confused manner, all human beings strive toward their own fulfillment. They tend to transcend what they are by becoming what they ought to be. It is for that reason, no doubt, that everyone aspires to love and to be loved. Unfortunately, where love is concerned, not everyone succeeds with equal good fortune. There are many who even fail completely.

1. *Emotional Cripples*

Men and women who have never had the chance to experience a love-communion are more numerous than customarily suspected. For some it is their excessive narcissism which acts as the obstacle to the existential fusion of their being with the being of another. Others are the victims of objective "barriers" extrinsic to their own personalities. But individuals in either group can experience only unhappiness, and the more refined their sensibilities are, the more they are bound to be unhappy.

After ten years of married life, Edward left his wife and children, to "begin life all over again" with another woman. When he was barely twenty years old, he had been engaged to a young girl who appeared to be passionately in love with him. Although Edward was in love with his fiancée, this did not prevent him from behaving badly, and with a lack of feeling, during the entire two years of their engagement. He caused his fiancée a great deal of unhappiness. The wedding night—to use her own expression—was "disastrous." He behaved "like a cad."

After that, relations between the young husband and wife only grew worse. To her great surprise, the wife gradually began to realize that it was not affection, but actually revulsion that she experienced in any intimate contact with her husband. Sexual intercourse became so painful for her at this point that she began more and more to refuse to have any.

Edward was a very sensitive man and suffered desperately when he realized that his wife did not love him. He thought he noticed signs of an affection for him on the part of a young girl who lived in the neighborhood, so he made her his mistress and then asked his wife for a divorce. Just as soon as the objective obstacle had been removed, however, and he found himself free to marry the young girl (with whom he said he was passionately in love) he began to adopt such a cruel course of action toward her that she had to break off relations with him. This left him more alone and more unhappy than he had ever been before. Edward could give no account of why he behaved the way he did, even to himself.

Edward had never really known any warmth or experienced the slightest ray of love in his childhood. His mother had died when he was very young, and he was brought up by his father's second wife, who played the role of the proverbial "stepmother." She evidently made his father's life unhappy, and she made life for Edward very difficult. In his adolescence, he tried desperately to find love. Although he was very virile, he adopted the coquettish manner of feminine behavior toward other people. He imagined he possessed irresistible charm and took pleasure in the imaginary thought that everyone who knew him admired him and liked him very much. His unconscious, however, was filled with fierce defiance against love. He was afraid of being disappointed. Deep down, like all who are deprived of love in their childhood, he did not believe that anyone could love him in any other way except the way his father had been loved by his second wife. As is almost always the case, his unconscious apprehension caused him to conduct himself in such a manner as to discourage anyone who seemed to be disposed to love him.

An individual's unconscious refusal to allow himself to be loved is sometimes not untainted with masochism.

Certain individuals—who are neurotic to a greater or lesser degree—derive pleasure from the suffering which their narcissistic solitariness creates for them. There are also individuals who reject any intimate relationship with another person because they feel they are too weak. They are afraid that if they submit to the influence of someone else's love, they may suffer the loss of their own identity. They are afraid that they will be unable to become anything except the other person's shadow. People with such weak personalities have very little aptitude for love.

Chantal was thirty-four years of age. She was haunted by the desire to get married. She was filled with horror and anxiety at the thought that she might never have the opportunity to realize her ambition. She was fairly attractive, and fairly well-off financially. Nor did she lack suitors. Her most recent suitor seemed to her to be endowed with all the qualities that were needed to make him a perfect husband according to all the standards in vogue in Chantal's social circle—standards that she herself accepted. She was convinced, moreover, that unlike some of the others, he was truly interested in her for her own sake, and not because of her money. But in spite of all her efforts and all her good will toward him, Chantal was unable to experience the slightest feeling of affection for this young man. She did not feel the slightest sensible or sexual attraction for him. Following the advice of individuals who said that "love would come later," she nevertheless became engaged to him. But when her fiancé gave her his first kiss, she experienced such a violent feeling of revulsion that she could not prevent herself from slapping him in the face and breaking their engagement. In despair over this new failure, she then had recourse to psychotherapy.

Chantal turned out to be the victim of a strong fixation on her father. She had adored him when she was a little girl. When she was an adolescent, she had been jealous of any woman in whom her father seemed to display any interest. When she was fifteen years old, she accidentally discovered him in an intimate situation with a friend of the family. The latter was half undressed and lying on the couch, with Chantal's father embracing her. Chantal experienced a violent reaction of resentment. She began to repress her affection for her father and to display a scornful indifference toward him. It was this repressed, humiliated affection, however, that had made it impossible for her to love any other man. It made her doubt her own sentiments whenever she happened to find a man attractive. Hurt by what she considered a betrayal on her father's part, she refused to believe in the possibility of a love without betrayal and disappointment. Not wanting to be betrayed again, her unconscious forbade her to fall in love. In the course of psychotherapy, however, Chantal first learned to understand her father, then to forgive him, and then to love him again with real filial love. Some time later she found herself in the position of being able to love another man in the way a woman should.

When love becomes impossible because of unconscious conflicts within the subject himself, psychoanalysis or psychosynthesis is almost always effective. Tragic in a different way is the plight of those men and women who are completely disposed to love, but who do not find anyone who loves them. Despairing of having their love requited, they often prevent themselves from obtaining the satisfactions that can result from a love that is not reciprocated.

Among women (much more than among men) frustration in love is the lot of those who have been made outcasts by nature—the homely, the deformed, the frail in health. There is such a thing, of course, as a "beauty in homeliness," a theme which Charles Plisnier has handled in an excellent way in one of his novels. For such beauty to be recognized, however, a whole set of particularly favorable circumstances has to be present together, or there has to be some unusual compensation in the nature of intellectual or artistic talent. Even in the case of the superior type of woman, a knowledge of her own homeliness usually engenders a strong feeling of inferiority. At the same time, this prevents her from appreciating the true value of the qualities which she does possess. It also prevents her from believing in love, at least as far as she herself is concerned.

There is a certain timidity in many men and women which makes it difficult, if not impossible, for them to establish the kind of relationship with other human beings that favors the development of a love-communion.

This sort of timidity is not necessarily the same thing as the fear of love which we shall be discussing next, although the former is sometimes a symptom of the latter.

In large cities in particular, the external obstacles encountered by the desire to establish an authentic existential communion with others are almost insurmountable. They stifle the very hope of finding love. Take a look at the crowd of lonely individuals, men and women both, who go walking by themselves in the park on Sunday. They stare at the couples they meet in sadness and envy. The very way they walk displays their feelings of lonely dejection. There is no reason for assuming that all of them are narcissists or that all of them are neurotic. The majority of them have come from out of town, either looking for a job or to complete their education. Timid and reserved by nature, they do not know how to go about making acquaintances. Some have more reason to complain than others. They are the ones whose sensibilities and tastes are far above the average level of those of the people they have to live and work with.

Francis, a minor employee in an insurance company, liked books and was interested in art and philosophy. Only the premature death of his father had prevented this gifted young man from going on to higher studies. If he had continued his education, he would have had access to a higher social level. The young girls with whom he worked were too mediocre and shallow to interest him. The only one whom he really respected, and secretly loved, was the director's secretary. His consciousness of the minor position which he occupied, however, prevented him from letting this elegant, educated young woman, who obviously received a better salary than he, even suspect his affection. He did not have the money to invite her out to a show with him. He was a lonely man in a crowd.

In any large city, men like Francis are legion. Women who suffer from the fact that no one loves them are even more numerous than men who find themselves in this situation. When men are lonely, they often find a substitute for love in the arms of a prostitute. Women do not have the same opportunities for having recourse to such a caricature of love. During the war, a large number of these unloved women in France allowed themselves to experience brief love affairs with American soldiers. The fact that they were fighting a war and were strangers seemed to make it all right for some of these women to grasp at a pleasure which their *superego* never would have tolerated their experiencing with their own country-men. The majority of them experienced disillusionment. They came to realize that this was no way to attempt to appease their hunger for love and affection. Most men also realize how deceptive their attempts are to break out of their intolerable loneliness by having sexual relations with a prostitute.

2. The Fear of Love

We have already indicated that timid individuals must not be confused with individuals who are afraid of love. Timid persons are inhibited, but it is not necessarily love itself that makes them afraid. As a matter of fact, it sometimes happens that their very lively desire to love and to be loved does make it possible for them temporarily to overcome their shyness. Among individuals whose unconscious makes them afraid of love there are some who are not timid persons in any sense of the term.

Irene, an office-worker about thirty years of age, was a fairly attractive girl. A number of men had made advances toward her, and she had had several offers of marriage. In her own thoughts and in conversations with her friends, she showed herself to be very desirous of either getting married or of taking on a lover, especially since she found life with her aged parents depressing. Whenever an occasion would present itself, however, she would experience panic and retreat. When the discrepancy between her desires and her actions was pointed out to her, Irene replied that her fear was explainable in terms of the disappointment which she knew several of her friends who had been married or who had taken on lovers had experienced. To listen to them, every one of them was unhappy. They bitterly regretted the loss of their former freedom. They found the sexual demands made upon them tiresome. Actually, however, this explanation was a rationalization of Irene's strong unconscious fear of sex. She deliberately never gave any thought to several of her friends whose love life was perfectly satisfactory. Once, when she was twelve years old, she had gone to visit one of her classmates. It turned out that her friend was not at home, but Irene was welcomed most cordially by her father. After he had gained Irene's confidence, he had her lie down on the couch, and attempted to violate her. She successfully defended herself, but the man had ejaculated upon her. This filled her with horror. Irene told the psychoanalyst that she never again gave any thought to this painful episode in her childhood until she remembered it in the course of an analysis of one of her dreams. That was the true and deeper explanation of her fear of love and sex.

Freudian psychoanalysts make much of what is called a castration complex to explain the cause of the fear of love in men. Neurotic individuals who were threatened in their childhood with "having it cut off" if they were not good, often imagine the female sex organ in the form of a dangerous abyss. Some of them attribute teeth to it, or a glutinous power which can enable it to imprison them.

The imagination in certain neurotic women terribly exaggerates the pain associated with defloration and with childbirth. This causes them to flee from love. Conclusions drawn from the observation of neurotic men and women, however, cannot legitimately be made to apply universally.

Sex is far from being the only source from which the fear of love springs. I know of men who are extremely avid of sexual pleasure and never lack occasions for indulging their desires, but these same men break off with a mistress as soon as they perceive a risk of their forming a sentimental attachment. The situation is the same in the case of certain women.

Mme. de R. was married for reasons of family convenience to a man she did not love and who, she said, had no personality. She was fond of making love, as she said, "just like a young boy." It might be with men who were friends of hers, or with just any man she met casually. She rarely remained for more than a few weeks with the same lover, even when their relationship was ideal. She was too afraid of becoming attached to anyone. Two or three times she had felt she was really in love, but each time she adopted a cold, aloof mode of behavior toward the object of her affection in order to discourage him completely from approaching her.

Mme. de R. had pretensions to the intellectual life. She explained her own behavior with respect to love and sex in terms of her ardent desire to maintain her independence intact. So long as she simply gave her body to a man, she thought she really was not giving anything but only taking her own pleasure, a pleasure which she compared with the great pleasure she also derived from eating and drinking. To give her heart along with her body, however, would have meant to lose her freedom. It would have meant becoming dependent upon her lover. That she did not want at any cost.

There was some truth in her own interpretation. Mme. de R. felt herself much weaker and more vulnerable than she pretended. She was therefore afraid that love would have the effect of dissolving her own fragile personality. I have observed the same thing in the cases of a number of men who were afraid of becoming attached to their sexual partner. So long as their relations with women remain strictly on the level of sex, they feel that they are dominating and "possessing" a woman. Love, on the other hand, would involve a surrender on their part to a woman. It would put an end to a superiority which they very much want to retain, but which their own unconscious knows is purely fictitious.

To return to Mme. de R., however, her fear of love was complicated by a number of other factors. The puritanical education she had received had taught her to have contempt for sex, and to see in it nothing but an ignoble stooping to animality. As a young girl, she had been very sentimental. She used to dream of love, but of a love that was completely ethereal and had no connection whatever with the body. Later on, as a result of the transactions that took place between the two families before her marriage, and the way her husband took possession of her on the wedding night, she acquired the feeling that insofar as she was a sexual being she represented the value of a piece of merchandise. It did not seem to her that what she called her deeper self was actually involved when she was enjoying a pleasure for which her husband had given her the taste, but with regard to which he gave her no satisfaction. She did not feel she was being unfaithful to her husband because she never refused him what he thought he had a right to. To be really in love with another man, however, would have struck Mme. de R. as involving her in real adultery. It would have obligated her to leave her husband and the enviable position in the world her marriage to him afforded her.

Mme. de R. was one of those innumerable victims of an education which tends to inculcate contempt for the body in general and for sexual activity in particular. Why have any respect for one's own or for anyone else's body if the soul alone is divine and the flesh something which is completely shameful and impure? This obviously is not what a puritanical education explicitly intends, but it is nevertheless the way in which many of those who have received its "benefits" feel about the matter in their unconscious. Not all of these individuals are neurotic in the technical sense of the term. The dangers of love are treated too often in both novels and sermons. The psychologist is in a position to realize that the repression of love is an incomparably more dangerous thing.

3. The Illusion of Being in Love

Which one of us has never been deceived about the true nature and the depth of his own feelings? Certain individuals, once they have experienced their first disillusionment, do not dare ever to believe in love again. There are some women who may not be frigid in any sense, who anxiously ask themselves continually—even when they are in their lovers' arms—whether or not they really are in love. They suspect it may be simply the power of auto-suggestion that is operating within them. There are some young women who are capable of giving themselves body and soul to a man whom they idolize and live for exclusively. They are no sooner separated from him, however, than they begin to doubt the genuineness of their own love. The origin of a phenomenon of this character is unquestionably neurotic. It is one of the forms in which the fear of love can make its appearance. The individuals are more numerous, however, whom no experience ever seems to teach, and who always interpret as true love what is only an illusory counterfeit.

The illusion of being in love is a common phenomenon among young people. They no sooner experience a slight sexual attraction, accompanied by perceptible emotion, than they consider themselves to have been blessed with a "grand amour." But they are usually not slow in coming to the realization that they have been the dupes of an illusion. In the case of men, such an illusion generally is dissipated as soon as they have taken physical possession of the woman without whom—so it had seemed to them —life would not make any sense. On the part of women, however, sexual relations tend to cause the illusion of being in love to persist. Sometimes they even act as the very cause that first gives birth to such an illusion. In our civilization at least, a woman becomes personally engaged in the act of sex to an infinitely greater degree than a man does. Frequently she obstinately holds on to her illusion in spite of contrary evidence, so as not to be obliged to admit to herself that she surrendered herself too frivolously. This is particularly true when the man in question is the one who deprived her of her virginity. The awakening will come much later, when it will be nonetheless painful.

It is not at all an easy task to set up a priori criteria on the basis of which to determine the distinction between genuine and illusory love. The subject himself is the one least of all in a position to teach us anything. Quite the reverse. Even when a prudent third party (who has been consulted about the quality of his amorous passion) believes there is sufficient evidence to warrant an unequivocal declaration in favor of illusion, the individual concerned almost always remains firmly convinced that the opposite is the truth. Even if he begins to have a few doubts about it, he will nevertheless try to persuade himself that he is not experiencing an illusion, but is truly in love with the other person. Nothing could be more normal, of course, since the illusion of being in love temporarily fulfills on the psychological level the same function that is assigned to genuine love.

The noted psychologist Wilhelm Stekel thinks that illusory love is "generally due to resentment. It always manifests an antagonistic tendency toward certain persons. ... It does not serve to appease one's need to love, but to hurt someone, to avoid defeat, or to procure any easy triumph for one's self."[1] My own observations

[1] *Frigidity in Woman in Relation to Her Love Life* (New York: Boni and Liveright, 1925), II.

confirm Stekel's in a general way. A young man from a good family was in love with a young girl of his own social circle and wanted to marry her. He learned that she preferred another young man to himself, a fellow who seemed to him probably much less deserving of her than himself. Frustrated in his love, the young man's pride was hurt. He became very unhappy. He was anxious, however, not to let his disappointment and unhappiness be noticed by others because he was afraid of being ridiculed by his friends and of being made an object of pity by his more successful rival. It was not long before he began to make a display of having relations with other girls. One of them was a working-girl, another a servant of his family, and a third a little, ignorant country-girl whom he met while on vacation. He tried each time to convince himself and others that it was a case of a "grand amour," and that he would not recoil before any obstacle to marry the object of his flaming devotion.

Every time I have had occasion to probe the deeper motivation of a lover of this sort, I have observed that it was primarily, if not exclusively, a case of wanting to show the other person who has been unfaithful to him that he did not care about her at all, and that "just anybody" at all could take her place in his affections. It is not at all surprising to find that such "love" turns out to be very fragile. Philosophers and psychologists both agree about the thoroughly ungenuine character of any behavior or sentiment that is based upon resentment. It makes no difference whether the relation to resentment is conscious or (as it generally is) unconscious. Sooner or later the subject who is experiencing the illusion of being in love will perceive that there was nothing positive in the feeling he had entertained for the woman of his choice. There will be two victims then, of one and the same illusion. If the two individuals are only lovers, separation will be a relatively easy matter. But frequently men and women who in principle are averse to marrying each other will marry the object of their illusory love with a surprising amount of ease. It is as if they wanted all the more to convince themselves and others of the strength of a flaming passion that has no fire under it. This is the tragedy of many marriages. We can only advise caution when individuals find themselves suddenly carried away by love a short time after a previous disappointment in love. In any event, they should not be too hasty about binding themselves to each other by means of permanent ties.

Emotional conflicts with one's parents are often at the root of an illusion of being in love. It is not possible to maintain that the prince can never love the shepherdess with a genuine love, or the cultivated young lady of high society her father's chauffeur. After what has been said about the insidious processes of the unconscious, however, it would only be right to recommend a great amount of prudence in such cases.

Dorothy, the daughter of an aristocratic diplomat, had just come of age when she informed her parents of her irresistible love for Luke, a very lowly subordinate of her father. She had been afraid of meeting with parental resistance, so she took the initiative about declaring her feelings to the young man. He would never have had the courage to take the initiative himself. It is not difficult to imagine the indignation of Dorothy's parents. They felt they would be disgraced by such a lack-luster marriage for their daughter. They tried to take advantage of her feelings of filial love and pretended that her foolishness could entail the risk of the ruination of her father's career. She did not yield. To force her father's hand, she became Luke's mistress, said she was going to have a baby (which was not true), and finally obtained not consent, but parental resignation to her marriage.

Scarcely six months of life together was enough to persuade Dorothy she had made a mistake. She had no profound interests in common with her husband. His education, tastes, and associations did not harmonize with hers at all. Unhappy and bored with the restricted life offered her by her husband, she fell into a nervous depression. In the course of psychotherapy it was disclosed that in her adolescence Dorothy had thought she detected an indifference toward her in the behavior of her father, whom she admired intensely. At seventeen, she had been hurt and disappointed because her father treated her friends with great gallantry but continued to treat her as a little girl. She even began to suspect that there was a liaison between her father and one of her best friends, one to whom she felt inferior in intelligence as well as looks. She did not think any more about it, and even forgot about her desire for revenge. Her unconscious, however, had neither forgotten nor forgiven. Nothing could have been more humiliating to the proud diplomat than a misalliance for his daughter. So Dorothy's unconscious suggested to her the illusion that she was in love with poor Luke.

I know of another case which is very similar to this one. Anthony was a well-bred young man who had a taste for art. At eighteen he fell in love with a friend of his mother's who was twice his age. He ardently pursued her, obtained her favors, and finally made her pregnant. None of this happened without the knowledge of his parents and of the woman's husband. He insisted that she divorce her husband and marry him. It was enough for his parents (who had taken the advice of a priest with "liberal ideas") to give their consent to this unusual arrangement for the young man's ardor to dampen immediately. In order to get out of an awkward situation, he enlisted in the army.

The reason behind his illusion of being in love seems to have been the intense jealousy he had experienced when he was ten years old because of the worldly, flirtatious kind of life his mother was leading. One time he became so angry that he spilled the contents of his ink-well over his mother's evening gown, thus hoping to prevent her from going out. Another time he ripped her lovely lingerie with a knife. For years he had given no further thought to the matter. He even showed himself to be completely indifferent as far as his mother was concerned. Here too, however, the unconscious selected its own form of revenge. It had to be something that would be particularly upsetting to his mother—the grotesque romance of her son with her own best friend!

Parents can do a great deal to prevent their offspring from having to experience the tragic effects of an illusion of love, effects which are so often directed against the parents themselves, even in a context that is not neurotic in its nature. It is wrong for them ever to want to control the emotional life of their children. There is a good chance that a young girl or a young man who is the victim of an illusion of being in love may see the flame die down quickly if he or she discerns that the parents are not too much opposed to it. In any case, it is never parental opposition which will prevent them from making a mistake. The reverse is true. It can even serve more or less to fan a flame that might otherwise have begun to flicker out of its own accord. I have observed this to be true in a very large number of cases.

Yet it is not altogether impossible for an illusion of being in love gradually to become transformed into true love. It happens so rarely, however, that it would not be correct to count on such an eventuality's occurring in the case of an individual known to be a victim of such an illusion. Only the discreet intervention of an experienced psychotherapist can make the subject aware of the illusory nature of his passion. Only the psychotherapist can get him to renounce it without any dramatic excitement or pain.

4. The Unhappiness of Love

No word is less precise in its use than the word "happiness." Whatever it may signify for different individuals, at any rate it is happiness that everyone expects to derive from love. Some individuals actually find it, although to many other persons love seems to bring unhappiness. This is especially true in cases when the education of the emotions has been almost totally neglected due to the rationalistic character of our civilization. Nothing could be further from the truth than the statement that "love is learned all by itself." Almost everyone will recognize that the art of love is also something that has to be learned.

It is not surprising that illusory love engenders unhappiness. It is not absolutely guaranteed, however, that genuine love will always bring happiness in its train. It sometimes happens that individuals who possess true love for each other are nevertheless made acquainted with suffering and unhappiness in their love-life. Other individuals may know happiness for several years, and then become unhappy in love.

The first condition for happiness in love requires that the love be favorable to the expansion of the personality of both partners, and that from the very beginning there exist between the partners a great harmony on both the physical and the spiritual planes. When this harmony does not exist, or when it exists on only one of the two planes, it is almost inevitable that love will engender more unhappiness than happiness.

When a man declares that he is unhappy in his love life, the chances are that the cause of it is his wife's frigidity. Frigidity is such a widespread condition that several experts on love think they are doing the right thing when they try to persuade men that they are wrong to attach so much importance to the "physical" pleasure which their beloved does or does not find in their arms. Let the man be content with enjoying his own pleasure! They cite the example of men of former times who, it seems, found it "shocking" for a respectable woman—for a wife, in other words—to desire and experience the intense sexual pleasure which characterizes the orgasm. Actually, those who give such counsel are either unaware of or underestimate the psychic factor in love. They are almost scandalized that a man is not content with a pleasure that is "purely physical," and by the fact that in desiring to give pleasure to his partner he is looking for a confirmation of his own virility. This is to ignore the extreme complexity of sex among civilized human beings. It is only in a very improper sense that either the feminine or the masculine orgasm can be called a "physical pleasure." A man and a woman who love each other tend toward a total existential communion, and sexual union is regarded by them, more or less consciously, as the mediator of such a communion. Under these conditions, why should anyone be astonished at the fact that the ecstatic pleasure which an orgasm can procure for a woman can take on so much importance for the one who loves her? It is true, of course, that there are less noble elements intermingled with the desire to "give pleasure," such as wanting to feel that the loved one is completely under one's own domination. But that also is human. The essential thing is that the will to power not eliminate completely the desire for communion.

At any rate, it is wrong to consider female frigidity exclusively from the standpoint of its relationship to the male partner. It is true that there is no need for a woman to experience an orgasm in order to be fertile. So long as they derive their happiness almost exclusively from accomplishing their vocation as mothers, it is possible for women not to be made unhappy because of the absence of sexual pleasure. But the modern, educated woman expects something else from a man besides the joys of motherhood. Still less is she content to look upon herself as simply an instrument of his pleasure. The modern woman is very much in favor of complete equality, and she senses in a vague way that complete equality cannot exist between lovers if only one of them takes and the other gives. There has to be mutual giving to insure equality. If, in the course of sexual intercourse, she does not experience a pleasure that is as intense as the one her partner seems to be experiencing, it is her partner whom she is ready to hold responsible for the "failure." As great as her love may be, it cannot prevent her from experiencing disappointment and from feeling contempt for her "impotent" partner. It is significant that many young women think that what is called impotence in a man consists precisely in his inability to give them pleasure.

In the beginning, the contempt of a frigid woman for her partner is only unconscious. It nevertheless undermines the feeling of admiration, which has a very important place in a woman's love. The frigid woman becomes nervous, capricious, quarrelsome. She is frequently in bad humor. This is not due just to the fact that she fails to experience the relaxation of her nerves that an orgasm would produce. Psychological factors again play the primary role. She unconsciously feels that she is the victim of an injustice and of humiliation. She has the impression of having been disappointed in her desire for perfect communion with the man she loves. She looks upon her husband as a selfish or an impotent individual. One day she will perceive that she is no longer in love with him.

Frigid women, more often than "passionate" women, are fickle. They go from love to love. Sometimes they actually find with another man the pleasure they were unable to find with a first. There is then a good chance they will remain faithful. Such women are frigid only in relation to a given man, but obviously this does not mean that the fault lies with him. The frigidity of a sufficient number of women, however, is "absolute." They are dissatisfied and unhappy no matter who the man is. Only psychotherapy can cure them of an infirmity that is almost certainly psychological in origin.

Frigidity in a woman is rarely congenital and seldom due to physical causes. It is usually the result of psychological conflict. Some of these conflicts go back to the subject's childhood, while others are related to her first experiences with love. Unfortunately, the majority of men are incapable of forming for themselves an accurate conception of the extreme importance which the gift of her body takes on in the psychological make-up of a young woman. Sexual tabus are anchored in the feminine unconscious much more strongly than they are in the unconscious of a man. The mystery with which her education surrounds sexual problems, and the overestimation of the significance of feminine virginity in current morality cause the virgin who gives herself sexually to the man she loves to see in this act a significance which far transcends the mere pleasure which, too frequently, is all her partner is interested in. The damage due to clumsiness or ignorance on the wedding night is difficult to repair, at least by the man who was at fault.

When it is not a question of neurotic inhibitions in the strict sense, but of inhibitions due to education and prevailing tabus, the initiating partner can do a great deal to prevent a woman from becoming frigid. He must know how to perform his role with an infinite amount of delicacy. In the first place, for example, it is not enough for a woman to know that she is loved. It is important that she *feel* it intensely. A man that is an intelligent lover will make sure to place himself in a position that will make her feel it. More detailed instructions along these lines can be obtained from several excellent books in existence which deal with the subject of sexual initiation.

Since a woman's initiation to love appears to be very difficult, certain sexologists believe they ought to discourage the idea of virgin-marriages in order to prevent unhappiness in love. They point to the example of several primitive civilizations in which defloration was entrusted to priests or relatives, but never to the husband. In our civilization, these sexologists expect the same "detraumatizing" effect to be produced by having recourse to premarital sexual intercourse. In my opinion, this is an oversimplification of the problem. For a civilized woman, it is neither possible nor desirable to separate sexuality and affectivity. The indispensable education and the battle against tabus owe it to themselves to tend in the direction that is likely to bring about a perfect integration of the two.

Jealousy spoils love almost as frequently as frigidity does. It deprives lovers of the happiness they had counted upon so much. In some cases, jealousy takes on the character of being clearly neurotic, while in other instances it can be considered something that is comparatively normal.

Gabrielle had married a lawyer who was a few years younger than herself. He gave her extraordinary proof of his love. In order to marry her, he relinquished his social position, abandoned his wife and children, and had to wait several years for a divorce. He was not a "woman-chaser" in any sense of the word, so she had no objective grounds for suspecting that he was unfaithful. She was aware of all this, and yet it did not prevent her from frequently creating violent scenes of jealousy. She supervised the visits of the women he had to see professionally. If one of them was younger or prettier than herself, Gabrielle suffered real torture. She went from a crisis of tears to insults and the smashing of dishes. Each day she searched her husband's pockets and portfolio, hoping to uncover "the evidence" of his unfaithfulness. She knew very well, however, that there was no such "evidence," since there had been no offense. Life eventually became unbearable for her husband. He no longer had any desire to go back to their apartment at night, so he would prolong his work at court or at the office for as long as he could, even though he realized that it would only be the cause of creating new and more violent scenes. Gabrielle knew she was in the process of destroying her own happiness along with her husband's, but her jealousy, she said, was stronger than she was.

There can be no doubt about the fact that Gabrielle's jealousy possessed a neurotic character. She knew this herself, so she finally decided to do something about it. Her jealousy appeared to be the fruit of a strong unconscious feeling of guilt. She felt guilty because she had married a divorced man, although on the conscious level she considered herself completely liberated from the principles inculcated in her in childhood by a Christian education. She also felt guilty with regard to her husband's first wife and children. Jealousy was the form of punishment that her unconscious had inflicted upon her. She would never be rid of it unless she decided upon a course of conscious reparation of her wrongdoings.

The case of Simon was equally neurotic. He suffered the pangs of jealousy with regard to the past life of his mistress, even though he knew he had "had" her as a virgin. Without the slightest evidence, he acccused her of having had numerous love affairs. He imagined that she still had many lovers. He even went so far as to accuse her, without the slightest indication, of belonging to a ring of "call girls." To the great detriment of his professional work, he spent hours every day and night supervising his beloved's goings and comings.

Although he was married and the father of several children, Simon had pursued this young girl ardently for more than two years. He had promised her he would divorce his wife. As proof that he wanted to marry her, he started the initial proceedings. She then became his mistress. Simon's conscience or *superego*, however, did not ratify his intention of abandoning his wife and children. In order to justify his eventual change of mind, the young girl "had" to be made to apppear to him to be unworthy of becoming his wife. His morbid jealousy originated, therefore, in a feeling of guilt which was related both to his family and his mistress.

The characteristic symptom of neurotic jealousy is the absence of any objective motivation. At other times, there may be a completely abnormal disproportion between the degree of jealousy and what might turn out eventually to have been a just reason for it. A woman may see the man she loves in pleasant conversation with another woman, for example, and conclude from this that there is a love affair between them. Jealousy that relates to the past life of a person with whom one is in love also has to be considered neurotic, even when the reproachable facts are true.

When jealousy is related to present facts and is motivated objectively, it can be looked upon as being normal. One may protest that he does not pretend to have any rights over the individual whom he loves, but the truth of the matter is that it is extremely rare for a love-relationship to be completely divorced from certain proprietary attitudes. In André Malraux's *The Human Condition,* Kyo and May enter into a compact to allow each other the most complete freedom with respect to love on the sole condition that each be absolutely frank about it with the other. When May tells him that she has had a lover, however, Kyo cannot prevent himself from suffering because of the fact.

CHAPTER SEVEN

LOVE AND AGGRESSION

PHILOSOPHERS AND theologians of former times used to consider the disorders and visible discrepancies in the world as a kind of scandal for the mind. They therefore directed their efforts toward pointing out, and trying to establish, that a universal harmony existed in spite of all. It is undoubtedly due in large measure to a reaction against this tendency, that modern philosophers since Hegel not only declare that there is no universal harmony, but conceive human relationships themselves fundamentally in terms of conflict. They have reached the point of attempting to justify the old adage, *homo homini lupus*. In our own era, the thesis that enmity and hate are more "natural" than friendship and love has found its most consistent and most brilliant advocate in Jean-Paul Sartre.

Sartre declares that when the subject becomes conscious of the existence of the other, it is in no way a cause of joy for him. As a matter of fact, he immediately perceives him as being a limitation, or rather a negation, of his own freedom, of his own *être-pour-soi* (being-for-itself). So long as he finds himself exclusively in relation to the world of *en-soi* (in-itself), man is in a position to look upon himself as the absolute subject, with unlimited freedom. It is enough for him to perceive another looking at him for him to realize that he himself is being regarded as an object. For the other person, he is not a *pour-soi*, but simply an *en-soi*.

Since the other person is depicted as a hostile force, the only spontaneous attitude one can adopt toward him is to engage in battle against him. It is necessary to deprive him of his character of being a *pour-soi*, a subject, and to make an object of him. This is the only way one can affirm his own character as a subject and a

132

pour-soi. Sartre explains indifference, sexual desire and hate as being the three principal means to which one has recourse to be able to effect the necessary refusal to recognize the other. Unfortunately, it is not always practicable: the other imposes himself on us and forces us to take account of him. Sexual desire, to be sure, reduces him to the role of a mere object, but its duration is ephemeral. Moreover, the other can respond in kind to our desire by his own desire. He too can make an object of *us.* The most effective of the three means would appear to be hate. Its goal is the annihilation (*anéantisation*) of the other. Not hate in its pure state, however. The other could defend himself against that. But hate disguised in the form of love. And this shows itself to be a weapon that is the more effective against the other as it incorporates within itself that form of aggression which is an essential ingredient of sexual desire.

In the perspective of Sartrean existentialism, therefore, love is not a unique psychological reality. It is especially not a creative force. A disguise for hatred, it tends toward the domination and the enslavement of the other. It does not attain its goal without difficulty, however. Everything would be simple and easy if I alone were able to love. By loving, I would reduce the other to his *être-en-soi,* to a passive state of being an object. In that way I would force him to restore to me my character of being a pure subject. Unfortunately, I would only be delaying recognition of the fact that the one I love is capable of loving me in return, of tending toward the same kind of affirmation of his own character as a pure subject, and consequently toward my enslavement and my reduction to the status of an object. Contrary to common opinion, mutual love is therefore not a source of joy, or in the best interest of the person. Far from a reconciliation through communion, mutual love is manifestly and fundamentally a combat, a mutual will to destruction and enslavement. Whether it is a question of the violence of "normal" amorous embraces, of practices of a sado-masochistic nature, or of the most tender caresses, it is all nothing but a case of weapons for combat. The bed of love is an arena in which implacable foes confront each other directly.

The greatest weakness in the existentialist theory of

"l'amour-combat" is the fact that it is not based on psychological experience. Like his master Heidegger in this respect, Sartre makes a pretense of being existential about what is, in reality, only the result of speculation and rash generalization.

If one limits himself strictly to observation of the concrete in a way that the proven techniques of depth psychology make possible, it is evident that love is not hatred in disguise, thanks to the bad faith of a cunning unconscious. It is undeniable, however, that it is not enough for two people to be in love with each other to insure that perfect harmony will prevail between them. A certain amount of aggressiveness is to be encountered in the majority of love relationships. In people who are fairly healthy psychologically, this is only an affirmation of each one's individuality, and it tends to make for a communion harmonious in the extreme. In neurotics, however, aggressiveness easily degenerates into warfare. It then resembles Sartre's descriptions readily enough.

As we know, the neurotic is a person who is very unsure of himself. For that reason, he is extremely jealous of his independence. He is afraid of being dominated by the one whom he loves. To protect himself, he takes the initiative and tries to dominate the person whom love entrusts to him. The other person can submit passively to his will to domination. In that case there will be no conflict. There will simply be tyranny. If a person's ego is normally strong, however, there is little chance that he will submit docilely to the tyranny of his partner. Passive submission can scarcely satisfy, and instinctively there is a tendency to offer resistance and counter-attack. When the neurotic will to dominate and the neurotic fear of being dominated encounter each other in two partners, amorous aggression easily degenerates into a sado-masochist combat. "No one," writes Simone de Beauvoir, "is more arrogant with respect to women, more aggressive or contemptuous, than the man who is uncertain of his virility. Those who are not intimidated by their counterparts are also much more disposed to recognize a counterpart in a woman." Similar remarks can be made about women. Those who for any reason whatsoever do not accept their femininity are vindictive, and unconsciously they employ all their ingenuity to instigate a battle.

However—and this is a methodological principle of extreme importance—observations made with respect to neurotics do not entitle us to extend our generalizations to the human condition as such. An abyss separates the normal aggressiveness between lovers from the warfare existing between lovers who are neurotic. A confusion of the two would be a serious mistake. A number of Freudians actually confuse neurotic aggressivity and the normal assertion of the ego. The man or the woman who wants to become "somebody" in the world and who makes the necessary efforts to attain his goal, is not being aggressive, even if he has to engage in combats.

Lovers who enjoy normal psychological health do not tend, either consciously or unconsciously, to subjugate the other person. They recognize the autonomy of his own ego, and they aspire to realize a communion between two freedoms, between two equalities, as being of the very essence of love. Such communion presupposes that each partner remains genuinely himself. It implies, therefore, a certain amount of aggressiveness. There is harmony between those who love each other, but it is not a static harmony. It can rather be described as a *dialectical* harmony.

The psychologist sometimes has to remain silent in a realm in which things are rarely simple. Whenever he succumbs to the Cartesian temptation to ideas that are "clear and distinct," he runs the risk of letting reality escape him. A number of depth psychologists, following Jung and Stekel, have established the bi-polarity of the majority of our instincts and feelings. Every instinct and every feeling has its opposite, which restrains what would otherwise be its excessive demands. Moreover, viewed existentially, none of our feelings or instincts appears to be absolutely "pure." It is always a situation of *complexes,* composed of feelings and instincts that are contrary but at the same time complementary. It would be wrong, for example, as Stekel has shown, to consider hate the negation of love. It is indifference, rather, which is love's negation.

Whenever two married people tell me they hate each other or cannot stand each other, I never altogether despair of succeeding in patching things up again after eliminating the source of their conflict. On the other hand, when there is no longer any resentment or aggressivity in at least one of the partners, but only indifference, then neither the efforts which the other person can make to "change himself" nor the advice and help of the psychotherapist is of any avail.

A certain person may make a show of a great deal of aversion for another person. He is completely persuaded of the sincerity of his feeling, or rather of his regretting it. It happens often enough, however, that upon digging a little more deeply into his psyche, one discovers that his aversion is only a weapon to defend himself against a particularly strong amorous attraction which, for precise reasons of a conscious or an unconscious nature, he rejects. This was the case with Arthur. His family wanted him to marry a wealthy neighbor, and he himself saw the advantages in a union which would enable him to put all his material cares aside. But he said his aversion for the young lady was such that he could not even conceive the possibility of living with her, much less sharing his bed with her. In the course of psychotherapy, however, it came to light that Arthur was in love with this girl ever since his adolescence. But he always felt terribly inferior to her, both socially and intellectually. Since any union between them had seemed impossible, he repressed his love, while his unconscious succeeded in constructing an effective system of defense in the form of a physical aversion. The defense worked, even though it is evident there was no serious obstacle on the side of the young girl. Contrary to the thesis so dear to Sartre, here is a case in which hate serves as a disguise for love.

It is true that the contrary also exists. I knew a young woman named Helen who thought she was "madly in love" with her cousin, who was fifteen years older than she. She took the initiative in becoming his mistress, and then married him in spite of all the protestations of her family. A short while after her marriage, she became melancholic, ceasing to be interested in anything at all, but particularly in anything that was either proximately or remotely concerned with her husband. She also became completely frigid in sexual relations, although before the marriage she seemed to take a very lively pleasure in them. Analysis revealed that Helen had always experienced a very strong instinctive aversion for this cousin, who was repellent to her both physically and morally. As a little girl, she often had been punished by her parents for having been too "mean" to him. One New Year's day as her cousin kissed her on the cheek, she bit him so deeply as to make him bleed. Her mother, who liked her cousin very much, gave her a beating. Little by little, Helen succeeded in repressing her instinctive aversion, which caused her too much trouble, and arrived at the point of persuading herself that she was in love with him. In reality, nothing had changed in her feelings. Here love was nothing but an effective unconscious disguise for hate. With astonishing dexterity, she had to make love serve the purpose of attaining the goals of her hatred. In marrying him, she in effect rendered her cousin very miserable. She would certainly have destroyed him if circumstances had not led to another conclusion: a separation between the two ill-mated spouses.

"The more one loves a mistress, the more one is on the verge of hating her," observed La Rochefoucauld. Obviously I do not share the famous moralist's pessimism, but my entire experience as a psychologist recommends a certain mistrust with regard to a love that is too demanding. Such a love is rarely content with a simple—and positive—confrontation of existences. It almost always tends in the direction of warfare, toward the subjugation if not the destruction of the other person. Adler, reacting against the pansexualism of his teacher Freud, was undoubtedly right when he drew attention to the fact that very often the *libido* itself is only a means at the service of the will to dominate. But Adler also sinned by excess against the spirit of a system in reducing all love to a simple manifestation of the will to power. The psychological universe is more complex than that.

CHAPTER EIGHT

MARRIAGE, THE ENEMY OF LOVE?

"WHAT A strange invention, marriage! And what makes it seem stranger still, is the fact that it is considered a spontaneous step. . . ."[1]

"The difficulty is this: Love and amorous inclination are altogether spontaneous, whereas marriage is a decision. Amorous inclination, however, has to be awakened with marriage and with the decision to want to get married. This means that what is most spontaneous must at the same time be a decision that is most free. What, because of its spontaneity, is so inexplicable that it has to be attributed to divinity, must at the same time take place by virtue of reflection, of a reflection, moreover, which is exhaustive enough to result in a decision. In addition to this, one of these things must not take place behind a mask, but everything has to take place simultaneously, both things have to be present together at the moment of climax . . . (But) reflection is the angel of destruction of spontaneity. . . ."[2]

These quotations drawn from the writings of Soren Kierkegaard—in spite of the rather grim jargon affected by the founder of existentialism—express the problem in an excellent way. The difficulty lies in trying to reconcile marriage with love. Henri de Montherlant, who disdains to interest himself in "what is ordinary," considers marriage disastrous for the superior type of man in a very special way, and not just because it would tend to make him bourgeois. It strikes him as a grotesque idea to picture someone as having said he was going over to have dinner with "the Dantes," for example. There could not be, and there should not be, a "Mrs." Dante.

[1] Soren Kierkegaard, *In Vino Veritas*.

[2] Soren Kierkegaard, *Remarks on Marriage*.

Criticism of the institution of matrimony is not only of recent date. Friedrich Engels, the friend and collaborator of Karl Marx and an approximate contemporary of Kierkegaard, wrote a scathing indictment of it from the standpoint of sociology. In spite of the fact that some of his observations were very correct, the analyses of Engels, like the analyses of all those who approach the problem of marriage with sociological prejudices, remain superficial. The strict parallelism he attempts to establish between the condition of the proletariat and the condition of women, for example, can hardly stand up under scrutiny. It is also fanciful to expect a complete transformation of the relations between men and women to result simply from a transformation in modes of production. Economic equality may appear to be an excellent thing. But as numerous examples serve to indicate, it is hardly enough to bring about, *ipso facto,* the equality of the sexes. The equality of the sexes itself—the necessity for this is unquestionable—is not enough to insure that all of the conditions required for happy love will be present together.

Without disdaining or underestimating the findings of sociology, the psychologist owes it to himself to approach the various problems that arise in connection with marriage from the point of view of the profound subjectivity of the human person.

1. The Separation of Marriage and Love in the Past

In the past, and for a very long time, it was something unusual for anyone to be interested in love in connection with marriage. The man or his parents chose the girl he would marry on the basis of strictly objective criteria, such as money, family, and so on. Among workers and peasants, special attention was given to the question of health and of fitness for work. In many cases, physical beauty was hardly taken into consideration at all. Even today, in the less refined social circles where psychological eroticism is almost non-existent, the majority of the men seem to attach very little importance to their companion's charms. Sexual relations are conceived of exclusively in terms of the satisfaction of a physiological need. The personality of one's partner appears to be a secondary consideration. Right up until recent times, men in high society followed the example of the "Sun-King," Louis the Fourteenth. There was the Queen of France, whom he had married for reasons of state. All he wanted from her was to insure the perpetuation of his dynasty. For pleasure and comfort, there were the Montespans and the Maintenons. The middle-class male also used to consider love and marriage as being in two very distinct compartments of life. It was completely by chance if they happened to coincide. My own grandfather used to speak with a mixture of irony and envy about one of his friends who "loved his wife the way a man loves his mistress."

It used to be very rare for women to be able to exercise any free choice in the matter of whom they were going to marry. In the nature of things, a certain promiscuity always existed among the lowest classes, but elsewhere young girls knew little or nothing about the man they were expected to marry. They evidently hoped for "happiness" in their marriage, but the education they had received forced them to think concretely of such happiness in terms of children and the performance of their duties as mistress of the household. They certainly also dreamed of love, since the romances they read spoke of nothing else. Once they were married, however, it could not have taken them long to realize that the love of their dreams bore no relation whatsoever to their condition of being a wife. In addition to this, sexual pleasure itself was considered a shameful thing for a respectable woman to enjoy. She simply had to perform her "conjugal duties." Ever since the middle ages, of course, there has been such a thing as courtly love. It was a subject still very much in vogue among novelists just prior to the First World War. Courtly love was always addressed to someone else's wife, however, since one's own wife was, by definition, incapable of becoming the object of erotic love.

This is not a book about morality. Therefore, it is not relevant here to express approval or disapproval of the customs of former times. They are of interest to us only to the extent that they enable us to comprehend more clearly today's psychological problems. It has to be admitted, however, that the customs in vogue in the past seem to have been satisfactory to the persons living at the time. It proves how profound is the transformation which has taken place in recent decades in the psychological structure of the men and women of our civilization.

It is not necessary to agree with Lévy-Bruhl and Sigmund Freud, and to assume the existence of a primitive human consciousness of an almost completely gregarious nature, in order to maintain that our ancestors spontaneously felt themselves to be members of the social group to which they belonged. They felt this just as much, if not more than, they felt themselves to be individuals. Nor is it necessary to point to the civilizations of Africa and Asia to illustrate the existence of a collective consciousness even in our own time—it seems to be very strong among the German and the Russian people. The institution of marriage, as it still exists officially today, was established because of the exigencies of such a consciousness—one in which the importance of the collectivity is greater than that of the individual.

It is safe to conjecture that it must never have been very agreeable for a man to have to live with a wife for whom he felt no personal affinity. It seems, however, that the majority of men resigned themselves to it without much trouble. Such resignation undoubtedly must have been easier for as long as the exclusiveness established by custom between a man's world and a woman's continued to be rigid. The perennial British custom of restricting clubs to men only is one of the many survivals in our own day of an age when men could not conceive of any friendship worthy of the name unless it was strictly between men. It was not so long ago that the ordinary Frenchmen spent their leisure time at the café or on the bowling green while the women chatted with one another before the doors of their homes. The conjugal relationship was pretty nearly limited to what went on in bed. In the upper classes of society, it sometimes did not extend even that far, since it was considered good form for man and wife to have separate bedrooms.

The entire set of customs that are associated strictly with the degree of evolution attained by human consciousness has to be kept in mind to prevent one from being too severe in his condemnation of a moral code that looked upon procreation as the sole end of sexuality. It is true that it also tolerated the "appeasement of concupiscence," but the very term connotes complete contempt for those who might have recourse to sex for such a purpose. Even today, there are certain pious people who will accuse themselves in confession of "having had pleasure with (their) husband." There are some women who would not dare approach the communion rail on the morning after they have had sexual intercourse with their husband because they look upon intercourse as something impure and imperfect, if not exactly sinful. It is wrong to accuse Christianity of being responsible for such a moral code. It constitutes all the more reason, however, for having to regret the fact that Christianity has not succeeded sooner in liberating men from the servitude which had been imposed on them for such a long time before the advent of Christ.

2. *The Present State of Confusion*

A profound transformation of western consciousness has taken place in imperceptible stages. Men less and less feel themselves members of a collectivity and more and more autonomous individuals. Right up until the time of the First World War, even in France, the feeling of national solidarity was still very strong. Even such universalist poets as Péguy and Valéry were ardent patriots. Patriots of their sort hardly exist any longer. The lower middle classes, especially in the rural areas, still display a degree of a touchy kind of nationalism, but if the surface is scratched, it is seen as simply an alibi in bad faith to cover up other interests that are less pleasant to talk about. Until quite recently, the proletariat always had a strong collective consciousness. It was a class consciousness, however, rather than a national consciousness. But there are indications that even here the quasi-mystical ties of the solidarity of yesteryears are being loosened, and each individual is beginning to experience himself more and more explicitly as a unique person.

It is not one of the psychologist's tasks to pass judgment on the value of the profound modification that has occurred in the consciousness of western man. It is his task, however, to take note of it, and to draw from it the consequences he sees it to have for concrete behavior. But there seems to be no reason why the moralist or the sociologist—though both of their disciplines possess a normative character—ought to interpret the psychological revolution which has occurred as a catastrophe. It is true that the individualism which has taken the place of a collective consciousness carries with it certain serious dangers. But there are many signs today that already presage the emergence of a new form of consciousness, which can be called a communal consciousness. This new form of consciousness stresses equally the individual and interpersonal communion.

But let us return to our subject. Not so long ago women were very proud of their mission to be the servants of the species. Today they are conscious of themselves as *persons,* and desire for themselves all that goes along with being a person, namely, independence, freedom, the right to happiness and the right to individual development. Men have been animated for a long time by the same desires, but from now on they will not be able to satisfy these desires except in relation to those of their feminine companions. Both men and women are beginning to assert more and more explicitly that the institution of marriage, as it has existed in its traditional form, is not very well adapted to this new state of mind. Priests, psychologists, doctors and other recognized counsellors know how rarely it is possible today to say of marriages, a few years after they have been contracted, that they have been completely successful and that they have contributed to the further normal development of each of the two partners.

For the majority of men, marriage is not an end in itself. They expect to find self-realization in professional, intellectual and political activities, or in activities of some other, similar nature. Depending upon whether or not the marriage has been successful, it can be a help or a handicap to such activities, without their depending upon it entirely, however. Women look at the situation in a different light. It is true that they are conscious of their own personalities, and that they aspire to their individual happiness and self-realization. But the majority of them expect to find all these things in marriage. Marriage still appeals to the vast majority of women, including the intellectual and emancipated types, as the most rewarding career of all. As a result, young girls too frequently look upon marriage not as a means which affords them the opportunity of living with the man they are in love with, but as an end in itself. They agree that it is so much better, of course, if the man who is going to serve them as a means toward their own self-realization is in love with them and they with him. This state of mind undoubtedly is at the source of a great number of disappointments in marriage on the part of women who are no longer capable of being "good wives" in the old-fashioned sense of the terms.

It is relatively rare that married life is not prejudicial to the complete personal development of a woman. Women who marry for love experience a greater fulfillment on the affective plane, where sex plays a great role. A normal love life is very difficult, of course—if not impossible—for women who are not married. It develops under the sign of sin even for the majority of those women who consciously refuse to recognize the validity of traditional morality. Add to this the fear of having an illegitimate child, and the fear of the social stigma which still usually acts as a restraining influence on the sexual freedom of the unmarried woman except on the lowest strata of society. Once a woman is married, she no longer has to contend with any sin or any fear that is calculated to make a mess of her love life. Since this is of such primary importance existentially, it is understandable why the desire to get married is so intense in young girls. It is also understandable how the status of being a married woman can appear so enviable in comparison with the status of being an "old maid." In addition, unless a person who is unmarried clearly possesses an exceptional personality, she is given very little (if any) social consideration in our world.

It is important, however, to emphasize the fact that the affective expansion just referred to can be realized only in a marriage that is based on genuine love. It is also essential that conflicts and unconscious inhibitions not outweigh what is permissible according to the moral code or the custom of the community.

As emotionally satisfied as many married women may be, if they have attained to a consciousness of their worth as individual persons, they still find it impossible to be content with emotional satisfaction alone. Husbands also no longer consider it enough for a woman to be an excellent, loving wife, although they do not appear always to be conscious of desiring anything else. The psychologist who has had to come to the assistance of the innumerable husbands and wives who have been disillusioned by married life realizes that in every case they have hoped for a total existential communion in marriage and failed to find it. The usual occupations and preoccupations of a young married woman leave her little time and energy for all the other interests in life. Emotional happiness itself turns her attention away from them. I have known few of my former students—then brilliant, cultivated, and intensely alive mentally and spiritually—who were still capable of rising above the banalities of daily life after ten or twelve years of married life, or with whom a prolonged conversation could be of any interest. The most frequent exception to the rule was to be found in the case of those whose married life had been a failure from an affective point of view.

Many households are broken up or disunited because of the absence of a genuine communion between husband and wife. Since he is in the habit of discussing with his wife only the children and various domestic problems which interest him only in a superficial way, it is not surprising that a man should find the company of another woman much more agreeable. The other woman may not always be more intelligent or more cultivated than his wife. But a man may find that with her he can talk about subjects on a different level. This is particularly true when the other woman is well educated and unmarried, when she is "well-informed" about the important problems of life to a much greater extent than a married woman of her own age and intellectual capacity. Even another woman who is someone else's wife can often give a man the impression of being more profound and more open to ideas than his own wife, for the simple reason that he does not have to share his daily life with her. Almost imperceptibly, a man may find himself becoming estranged from the woman he thought he would love always. Even if he does not leave her, he may begin to see himself as living alongside of her rather than together with her.

It would be a mistake to consider the woman alone responsible for the failure of conjugal love. She frequently suffers from the lack of a deep communion between them as much if not more than her husband suffers from it. And it is she who frequently takes the initiative in breaking up their relationship. In the beginning, the joys of love and motherhood combine to overwhelm her to the point where everything else may seem to be very unimportant to her. Sooner or later, however, she too begins to become aware of the other needs of her whole self. She would like very much to be able to communicate with the man she loves on the intellectual, the esthetic and the spiritual planes. She would like him to talk to her about what he is doing and thinking. She would like to participate with him in Life with a capital "l." To her sorrow, her husband steals away from her or listens to her with only one ear. Too much conversation about the small problems of family life causes him to doubt that his wife can be interested seriously in such matters as international politics, social reform or current intellectual problems. And it is frequently true that she is not *au courant*. Perhaps it is the fault of her husband, who never takes the trouble to talk with her about such things. So many wives of "superior" men become acquainted with the ideas, opinions and various interests of their husbands only because they hear them spoken about at social gatherings. It is impossible to get him to speak about them at home, just for the sake of the interest of his wife.

John and Annette had been married for eight years. At social gatherings, he was a brilliant conversationalist, very jovial and very much the man of the world. He was admired because of the extent of his knowledge. Annette had a certain elegance, but also a great receptiveness toward anything great and beautiful. The men who spoke with her could not help comparing her to their own wives, who seemed to them to be "so ordinary." They envied the happiness of the man who was the husband of such a woman. The women, naturally, thought that Annette was very lucky to have such a man as John for a husband. They thought it impossible for her ever to be bored. After I had become a confidant of this seemingly ideal couple, I found out that their home life was a completely unhappy one. At home, John was sulky and tactiturn. For several years, he had been lacking not only in kindness, but even in elementary politeness toward his wife. He never spoke to her about any of those things which made him so appealing outside the home. Annette at home was not the elegant, outgoing woman known to her friends. She besieged her husband with recitals of domestic cares and woes. She constantly complained about the children and the neighbors. John remembered, though, that during their engagement, Annette had been the most remarkable companion ever. Whose fault was it that this marriage turned out to be such a failure? Undoubtedly it was the fault of each of them. More especially, however, it was the fault of the lack of adaptation of the institution of marriage to the new structures present in the psychological make-up of the modern human being.

It has been suggested by some that the lack of harmony which prevails between the institution of marriage and the new state of individual consciousnesses might be remedied by recommending engagement in some form of professional activity for all married women. It is an unquestionable fact that women who engage in a profession that is fully suited to their tastes and capacities are hardly ever subject to the sort of danger we have just been discussing. Marriage does not make them ordinary. It does not limit their horizon. But, unfortunately, it is impossible for the majority of women (as it is for most men) to be able to engage in such a profession. In addition to that, the training which young girls receive, even at the present time, hardly tends to make them seek their individual self-realization in a profession. That is why most of them prepare themselves for a profession in a way that is too superficial to enable them to take any true interest in it. The fact that the majority of women who work have also to take care of a home and children at the same time is something else that must be taken into account. The result, almost inevitably, is a permanent state of agitation and strain which is hardly conducive to the development of any depth of communication between husband and wife.

3. Marriage and Children

In former times, children were considered the essential element in marital happiness. As we have seen, men as well as women frequently married in order to have children. It was with this end in view that they chose a partner. But after what has been said about the evolution of consciousness, it should come as no surprise that today children no longer hold the first place with regard to the choice of partner and with regard to married life itself. Instead, they frequently appear to be a threat to the love between husband and wife.

However, there are still certain young women—even among the well-educated—who think about marriage exclusively from the point of view of its offering them the sole means approved by society and their own conscience of satisfying their imperious need to have children. Not all of those who speak and think in this way, however, are equally sincere.

Nicole was an intellectual, twenty-four years of age. She was a good-looking girl and in the best of health. She told me about the debate that was going on within her. She was actively engaged in a profession which she loved and which afforded her an easy life that was in every way suitable to her tastes—travel, books, etc. It would cost her a very great deal to have to give it all up. On the other hand, she experienced an ardent desire to become a mother. She wanted very much to have children of her own. But for this purpose she would have to marry. In her case, this would necessarily mean renouncing not only her dearly-prized independence but her profession as well. A little probing of her unconscious revealed to Nicole herself that the need she experienced so intensely was actually dictated by her strong erotic impulses. Her *superego,* formed by a combination of influences stemming from her education, her social environment and her religious faith, obviously had forbade her to think about the appeasement of her thirst for erotic satisfaction in any way other than in a marriage blessed by the Church and approved by society. Her *superego* would not permit her to admit even to herself that her body and her heart were longing for a man's love. The desire for motherhood served as a disguise for her real desires, which were not to be avowed.

In Mme. G., on the other hand, the element of erotic desire seemed to be completely absent. She did not remember having experienced the slightest sexual desire when she was a young girl, nor having had any occasion even to ask any questions about sexual problems. After she married, she willingly met the needs of her husband, whom she loved, but she herself never experienced any desire or pleasure. From the time she was an adolescent, her most ardent desire was one day to have a great number of children. At thirty, she actually was the mother of six children. They gave her a great deal of work and trouble, but she found intense happiness in the midst of it all. She never complained about the great fatigue brought on by her pregnancies, or about the fact that her heavy domestic duties required her to forego various pleasures. Mme. G. had had an exceptionally happy childhood, enhanced by the very great affection that existed between her parents. A profound, intimate relationship existed between her and her mother, of a kind that was neither exaggerated nor inhibiting. Her desire to have many children seems to have had its roots in her need to imitate her admired mother and to revive the intensely affective situation of her own childhood by repetition (her parents had also had a great number of children). She loved her husband very much. It was not so much as a sexual partner that she loved him, however, but as the father of her children.

As typical as the case of Mme. G. may be, in our time it is very exceptional. The vast majority of young girls do not marry any more in order to have children, even if, like Nicole, they say and think that they do. Like their mothers, it is "happiness" which they expect to find in marriage; but in their vague notion of happiness, it is the love of an erotic kind that evidently occupies first place. Depending on the situation, this eroticism is permeated to a greater or lesser degree by the spiritual.

It is not that young husbands and wives who are so aware of their own individuality and so desirous of finding their own self-development in marriage are opposed, in principle, to the idea of fatherhood or motherhood. Quite the reverse is true. In the majority of their homes, children are welcomed with joy. While the typical middle-class family of about thirty years ago made a cult of having only a single child, its sons and daughters have no objection, in principle, to having several children. Frequently they even have too many. The education of these children is much more intelligent than the kind of education they received themselves. There is unquestionably more emotional warmth between parents and children today than there was in former times.

Even Mme. G., however, who had married in order to have children, married the man she loved, that is to say, the man whom she wanted in a positive way to be the father of the children she would give birth to. On the supposition that Nicole will marry one day in order to be able to give free rein to her strong eroticism, the chances are good that she also will marry a man whom she loves. She will recognize in him, unconsciously perhaps, the appropriate sexual partner. A certain number of marriages are still "arranged" in certain traditionalist bourgeois circles, but even there it is understood implicitly that the two young people whose meeting was arranged will not marry each other unless they succeed in coming to the point of loving each other. It is true, of course, that too frequently—and especially in the case of young girls—the too ardent desire to profit from the advantages offered to a married woman creates an illusion of being in love. This inevitably entails disappointment and the unhappiness that was discussed in a previous chapter.

Children may be welcomed gladly as the fruit of love. But frequently they then become stumbling blocks in the path of marital love. Absorbed more and more by the care and education of the children, a wife finds it very difficult to remain at the disposal of her husband as much as she was during the first years of their union when there were only the two of them, or when there was only one baby in the home. In former times, husbands found this state of affairs completely natural, since they had married for the purpose of raising a family. Husbands today marry in order to have the woman they love *for themselves*. As a result, they experience disappointment and resentment. Sexologists maintain that motherhood is conducive to awakening feminine eroticism. Unfortunately, the sleepless nights spent with a sick baby and the numerous cares created by children of school age too frequently interfere in practice with the love life of husband and wife. The anxious, overworked wife ceases to be an object of erotic love. The relative detachment of the husband with regard to the children is resented by many women as a sign of a lack of love for themselves. This frequently results in their growing farther and farther apart from their husbands and centering their affection more and more on the children.

The psychologist frequently finds himself in the position of having to uncover the source of the spiritual estrangement between a husband and wife whose union unquestionably had been established on the basis of a sincere mutual love. In a great number of cases, the story is no different from that of George and Odile.

She was a journalist, he an engineer. Both of them were devout, militant Catholics. They wanted their marriage to be based on complete communion and perfect equality. Each of them interested himself in the professional activity of the other. They were in the habit of exchanging opinions on their respective problems and endeavors. After the birth of the first child, Odile continued with her journalistic career, having hired a woman to take care of the baby during the day. By force of circumstances, however, communication between husband and wife began to grow more rare and more superficial. When Odile returned home, she had to occupy herself with the baby instead of being able to throw herself into the usual lengthy discussions with George. He did his best to give his wife a hand, but like most men he was very awkward about the sort of things that had to be done. He got in her way and hindered her more than he helped her. So he finally took to sitting in an armchair and plunging into prolonged reading of newspapers and magazines while Odile went about her maternal duties. The birth of a second child the following year obliged Odile to give up her professional career and to devote herself completely to her home. In the beginning, the new arrangement seemed to be favorable to communion between husband and wife. Returning from work, George would find his wife much more relaxed and more at his disposal. She almost always had already finished her household chores and wanted nothing more than to spend several hours in spiritual and intellectual exchanges with her husband. But interesting subjects of conversation were much rarer now than when Odile had been involved in intense professional activity. In spite of the efforts she made to interest herself in the outside world as much as in the past, George sensed that her heart was not in it any more. More and more frequently, he came to prefer reading the newspapers and magazines to a conversation that never succeeded in amounting to a real exchange. Odile found it impossible to leave her children alone, there being three of them by this time. She had to forego the source of enrichment which the theater, the cinema and visits with friends had been to them both before. Without wanting to admit it, husband and wife became more and more bored with each other. George more and more frequently found excuses to prolong his absences from home.

The birth of several children had not caused any financial embarrassment to George and Odile, and they did not have to put up with the problem of small living quarters, which so many young couples have to face. The tears and cries of the children in a small apartment are frequently the cause of tension between husband and wife. They can drive the husband out of the house.

4. In-Laws

Whether they will it or not, the married couple realize that the marriage contract entails certain obligations and establishes certain bonds which may be difficult to reconcile with the spontaneous character of love. If it were a question of obligations only with regard to each other and the children, love would succeed in ridding them of the character of any restraint and imbuing them with its own spontaneity. It does not take long, however, for an individual to realize that he or she has married not only a wife or a husband whom they love, but frequently his or her family and its milieu as well. I know of several couples who were united to each other by ties of mutual love, but whose love was put to severe tests because either the one or the other of the married partners, and sometimes both, had not succeeded in becoming integrated into the family of the other party.

The classical conflict between daughter-in-law and mother-in-law has been handled very often by novelists and dramatists. Mothers are rare, especially mothers of an only son, who do not consciously or unconsciously look upon a daughter-in-law as the "stranger" who has committed the crime of stealing their son away from thèm. They are certain in advance that the daughter-in-law will not know how to take care of their "boy" as well as they themselves have taken care of him. To imagine that another woman could make their son happy seems to many mothers to be a kind of blasphemy against the eminent dignity of motherhood. When it is impossible for them not to recognize that the young husband is perfectly happy with his wife, their unconscious tends to interpret it as an ungrateful betrayal on the part of their own "boy." Instead of being pleased with such a daughter-in-law, the jealous mother holds more of a grudge against her than if she were making her son unhappy.

Mothers-in-law are not the only ones to create obstacles to the realization of marital love. The behavior of certain fathers-in-law with regard to their son-in-law is scarcely less indicative of a "complex." Mr. S.'s daughter married for love, and was perfectly happy in her marriage. She had married an intellectual who was already famous and who had a promising career ahead of him. Theoretically, he was the kind of son-in-law that should have enchanted Mr. S. since he himself was a man of great culture. Before he learned that this young man was going to marry his daughter, he actually appreciated him very much and was delighted to be able to treat him as a friend. As soon as the engagement took place, his feelings and his attitude changed. He set about finding a number of faults in the young man. He criticized him in front of his daughter for not being in a better financial situation, and reproached him for his inaptitude to meet the demands of real life. It was worse still after their marriage. The father-in-law no longer made any secret of his contempt for his son-in-law. The young wife unconsciously let herself be influenced by her father and finally divorced her husband. Her next husband was a rich industrialist who was in all respects the complete opposite of her first husband. Mr. S. was not satisfied with his new son-in-law either. He disapproved of his crass materialism and grossly ridiculed his lack of culture. Without being able to admit it, particularly to himself, he wanted to have his daughter all to himself.

Mothers-in-law and fathers-in-law like those whose image we have just drawn are legion. But in the majority of cases, it does not seem that one has the right to speak, as the Freudians do, of an unconscious incestuous love. More simply, their child—especially their only child—had played an immeasurably great role in their emotional life, and they cannot resign themselves to the fact of having to share his or her love with a daughter-in-law or a son-in-law. As numerous as conflicts between father-in-law and son-in-law and between mother-in-law and daughter-in-law undoubtedly are, the facts do not warrant any generalization. Although such cases may not come so often to one's attention, there are at least as many instances of in-laws whose behavior toward the husbands and wives of their children is free of all conflict, resentment and jealousy as there are cases in which these elements are present. The psychologist, more than anyone else, encounters situations which border on the pathological. The danger of professional distortion is therefore great in his case. He is apt to take the abnormal as the model of the normal.

The difficulty of adjusting to the social environment of one's husband or wife is much less serious in our time than are conflicts with one's father-in-law or mother-in-law. In any case, it is much less important than it was formerly, when social class distinctions were more rigid. In certain instances, of course, the environment still can weigh heavily upon individuals and actively contribute to the ruination of understanding between husband and wife.

Mr. and Mrs. V. were married as soon as he had completed his studies, while she continued with her studies at the Academy of Fine Arts. They were in love with each other. They both belonged to the same lower bracket in society. He figured that she would be a better help to him in furthering the realization of his ambitions than some girl from the upper middle classes. He planned to "climb high." Unfortunately, it did not take Mr. V. long to discover in his wife a total lack of interest in matters that were of concern to the people in the social group to which he belonged. She could not help comparing her husband's associates with the artists she had become accustomed to when she was studying. She found his acquaintances vulgar and unattractive. Her lack of sociability toward them became a detriment to his career, and

he held it against her. On his part, undoubtedly because
of an unconscious need for revenge, he could not tolerate
his wife's "Bohemian" friends. The couple finally broke
up, although their union had been formed under the best
auspices. Marriage is not only—nor even primarily—an
idyllic state of life. It is first and foremost a social
institution.

5. The Autonomy of the Individual Person

In the modern world men and women both are very
jealous of their independence. At the beginning of a
marriage, this is hardly given a thought. Man and wife
are disposed completely to share everything in common
with each other. They gladly believe that their life together as a couple will be so intense that it would be impossible
to regret the fact that the life of the individual has been
absorbed by it. The husband, of course, rarely renounces
his individual life. It is implicitly understood by him that
it is his individual life that will constitute the basis for
the life of the couple.

In the past the majority of the wives seem to have
adapted their own existence to that of their husband without difficulty and without any problems. The education
which the "better" young girls received hardly tended
toward the formation of their own personalities. Rather, it
was geared toward making them good wives and toward
preserving them from boredom. This is not so in the case
of the educated woman today. She has her own ideas and
her own preferences. She expects to contribute something
of her own as one half of the new existential reality constituted by the married couple. Many men accept this new
conception of married life in principle, but experience
shows that, in practice, things have not become any more
simple.

Custom dictates that husband and wife go out together
and that they have the same persons for friends. Frequently enough this does not present any difficulty. An
identity of tastes and interests may have been present as
an ingredient in their love from the very beginning. Such
an identity is in no way required, however, as a condition
for genuine love. Differences as frequently as similarities,
unless they are irreconcilably opposed, can serve to set off

the fuse of love. In particular, there are certain weak narcissistic individuals who are looking for a reflection and a confirmation of themselves in the other, while strong, well-balanced personalities are attracted more towards another individual who will be truly an Other— that is, someone with whom a real dialogue is possible. As a consequence, it is not without reservations that a great number of husbands and wives put up with the exigencies imposed by custom.

Isabelle and Marcel de B. had been married for twelve years. It had been a true marriage of love. They were both students of literature when they met each other at gatherings of young esthetes and "recognized" themselves in each other. They both continued to love modern painting and to read the same books. Each of them began to acquire new interests, however, which were not the same for both.

Marcel became passionately interested in politics. An active member of a political party, he liked to attend meetings. His best friends were men in politics. Isabelle was utterly bored by politics. In keeping with the social code of the milieu in which they lived, she felt she had to accompany her husband to his meetings, from which she returned completely exhausted and in a disagreeable, hostile humor. She had her husband's political friends to dinner and submitted herself to the ordeal of remaining in the living room with them for hours on end. Their discussions did not interest her at all, and it was painful for her to show herself as amiable as her husband desired her to be. This resulted in frequent disputes between husband and wife. At times Marcel would forego the gatherings and receptions which interested him to avoid imposing a disagreeable task on his wife. It was then his turn to be in a sulky mood. He would hold it against his wife that he had deprived himself in such a way.

Isabelle had for several years taken an interest in questions of a spiritual nature. She frequented certain Hindu circles, and she enjoyed having a certain "open-minded" Catholic priest pay her a call. She found his conversation fascinating. But how could she impose on her agnostic husband the ordeal of having to mix with such men and to attend such gatherings? It would displease him even more than his political meetings had displeased her. She tried to get him to become interested, but to no avail. She thereupon decided to give them up herself. It cost her a great deal and kept her from pursuing her own development. It resulted in intensifying her feeling of not being happy in her married life.

It was not without difficulty that I succeeded in making both husband and wife, whose respective desire for self-realization was endangering their marriage, admit that it had become imperative for them to break with the conventions of their social environment. It was finally agreed that each would pursue his own preferences freely and mix with those with whom he pleased. Contrary to what one might have feared would happen, it did not result in any emotional estrangement between them. Quite the reverse. Each of them now had the opportunity of expanding his own personality without having to look upon the other as being an obstacle to his own development. They became more understanding. She very graciously had her husband's friends to dinner from then on, while he allowed her to retire from the living room as soon as her duties as hostess were terminated. He no longer made fun of his wife's spiritual associates, since he was no longer expected to become involved with them.

I would hesitate to maintain that the solution which was so effective in the case of Isabelle and Marcel could meet all cases of a similar nature. It is unquestionable, however, that the educated men and women of our time are not in a position to find their happiness and personal fulfillment in marriage unless they succeed in reconciling their personal independence with the unity of their life together as a couple.

6. *Seeing the Whole Picture*

We have already alluded to the great difficulty which husbands and wives experience in trying to prevent themselves from being submerged by the ordinary details of daily life. It is undoubtedly here that the difficulty of reconciling marriage with love manifests itself in the clearest possible way. Lovers instinctively place the communion between themselves on an elevated ideal plane. The feelings they experience and the thoughts they communicate to each other tend in the direction of the universal and the essential. Every time they meet there are so many sublime things to recount to each other! Or if they content themselves with something less, it is their own love which becomes the subject of conversation between them.

In spite of the good will on the part of each of the partners, it is not possible to maintain married life at such a high peak. Each partner is in the presence of the other even when they have nothing interesting to say to each other and when they are overwhelmed by cares and fatigue. The feeling develops gradually that one's husband or wife is less susceptible of being moved by the great and beautiful things of life than a friend whom one sees from time to time when he has a positive desire to do so. In addition to this, how can one avoid repeatedly talking at the dinner table about the health of the children, or their mischievousness, about the price of steak or about the capriciousness of one's mother-in-law? Getting into the habit of talking about such ordinary matters, husband and wife finally reach the point of hardly ever touching on subjects of more universal interest. The longer they live together, the more they have the impression that they have said all there is to say to each other and that they know each other so well that there is no point in giving expression to what they think and feel.

How many husbands complain about the little interest their wives take in those things in which they themselves have a passionate interest, whether it be art, philosophy, politics, their profession, or something else? And wives complain that their husbands are not prepared to enter into any exchange with them on a profound level. They obviously prefer the reading of a newspaper to holding any intellectual or spiritual conversation with them. In educated circles, it appears that a large proportion of adulteries are explainable by the fact that husband and wife have not been able to prevent their relationship from slipping into banality. In the person of another woman, the husband meets the attentive and admiring companion he needs in order to retain his confidence in himself. Frequently it is the wife of another man. And this other man probably finds her, as far as he is concerned, just as little interested in "important problems." The wife, for her part, is happy to find that another man finds her intelligent, idealistic and charming. So much the worse if it is the husband of a friend of hers who has been trapped by the banality of her married life.

Mr. and Mrs. O. had been married for twelve years. They began to think more and more about the inevitability of a separation. He said that she was lazy and quarrelsome, and that she wasted her time reading "idiotic" novels and listening to records. She complained about having to live with a "barbarian," a "primitive man," who thought about nothing except how to amuse himself, and who was completely closed when it came to the life of the mind. I happened to make the acquaintance of several of their friends. I learned that Mrs. O. had the reputation of being a very charming and pleasant woman, whose conversation was sparkling. As for Mr. O., it seems that he was a completely remarkable man, not only because of the great openness of his mind, but also because of the great kindness and understanding of his heart. Mrs. O. was greatly surprised when I told her that I had had a very interesting conversation about classical music with her husband. She thought his only interest in music was in jazz. Mr. O. was no less surprised when I told him about the excellent reputation his wife enjoyed in the circle of their associates.

Husbands and wives are usually wrong when they think they know each other very well. Strangers often know them better. Mrs. Z. was annoyed by the unanimous praise bestowed upon her husband by their neighbors and acquaintances. She herself looked upon him as incompetent and selfish. Her efforts to persuade others to her way of thinking failed. Instead they judged her severely for speaking so badly about such a fine man. They pitied him because he had such a woman for his wife.

I obviously would not try to maintain that all of the complaints lodged against each other by husbands and wives are without foundation. Where married couples are wrong, however, is in each one's being so sensitive to the inevitable little failings of the other that they are not able to appreciate the true and the good qualities that still remain in spite of everything else. The other person's defects are only a part of the total picture. Husbands and wives frequently cannot see the beauty of the forest for the imperfections they notice in the trees. It is not impossible for this state of affairs to be remedied.

7. Marriage and Eroticism

In *Positions et Propositions*, Paul Claudel writes, "Love, the consent on the part of two free persons to give themselves to each other, appeared to God to be so great a thing that He made of it a Sacrament." Actually, the great problem at the present stage of the development of human consciousness is one of integrating eroticism into marriage or marriage into eroticism. In any case, the institution of matrimony has no chance of survival unless a successful integration of the two is brought about.

In our civilization, marriage offers (in many ways) the most favorable conditions for the erotic development of the partners. The legal ties of the marriage contract abolish the inhibitions which stem from the fear of unwed motherhood and of other social and moral prohibitions. The act which was looked upon as sinful and shameful before marriage henceforth is considered not only licit but—as moralists more and more frequently are coming to assert—almost holy. Certain theologians speak of coitus between husband and wife as a sacramental act which "opens up the floodgates of sanctifying grace." The cohabitation of husband and wife also makes it possible for them to discover each other's erotic resources much more easily than is the case with lovers, whose relations are by nature more occasional and less permanent. Actually, in many cases, a woman who was frigid in pre-marital sexual relations expands and loses her frigidity the moment she is married.

It is unquestionable, however, that it is precisely in this too perfect assemblage of favorable conditions that the worst pitfall for erotic charm also lies. We have insisted a great deal upon the fact that human eroticism is primarily psychological in character. It is also extremely complex. The unexpected, the new, the game of seduction, considerably add to the factor of erotic attraction, even in the case of individuals who assign first place to spiritual love in principle. In the sexual life of a married couple, however, it is difficult to avoid habit and routine. As a result of this, many men around the age of fifty, after twenty years or more of a happy married life, become partially or totally impotent with their wife. At the same time, they may experience a strong attraction toward other women who may not always be more beautiful or younger than the one they disdain. If they yield to temptation, they are apt to find (to their pleasant surprise) that they are as "potent" again as they were in their youth. The premature disappearance of erotic attraction between husband and wife does not necessarily mean that they do not love each other any more.

The French custom of the one marital bed is particularly disastrous for eroticism. A body which one is always touching, even when he does not want to, loses all its mystery and soon, consequently, all its attraction. Sexual relations are made too easy. As a result, they frequently take place without the desire for them being really intense and without erotic foreplay having been engaged in sufficiently. The natural result is an erotic pleasure of a very diluted character. In the last analysis, the instinctive impulse turns away from so stale a goal.

The same set of causes and conditions frequently operates to bring about frigidity in women who for years were very ardent in their sexual relations. After several years of married life, they complain about the fact that they experience nothing but boredom and fatigue in the arms of their husbands. It is true that frequently they simulate pleasurable reactions, in the false hope of thus better satisfying the needs of their husband and preventing him from turning to another woman. With husbands or wives, it is always a case of their conjugal love's being separated from eroticism and thus being exposed, by the very nature of things, to serious peril. As we have seen in the first chapter, to be authentic, love between a man and a woman has to be at one and the same time both physical and spiritual. It is only in old age, when the flesh no longer makes any demands, that the spiritual alone is enough to bind husband and wife solidly together. Such a transfiguration of their love, however, has to develop gradually and in a natural way. When sexual attraction disappears from love prematurely—and it will always be too soon as long as the sexual impulses have not been completely extinguished—it is difficult to continue to love one's wife or husband in a spiritual way for any length of time when one finds oneself reaching out in an erotic way toward some other person. But experience proves that between forty and fifty, at the age when (as we have seen) marital eroticism is in special danger, there is a vital resurgence of eroticism in many men and women. Normally at that age the man has attained the main objectives of his professional ambition, and the *libido* which was affected by it becomes susceptible. A woman, for her part, finds herself free of the numerous duties associated with the rearing of the children. The psychologist does not see anything but what is perfectly natural, therefore, in what, with a certain irony, is called the noonday devil.

Husbands and wives require solid moral principles and great strength of character in order to resist and overcome the erotic attraction they will inevitably experience for another woman or another man when habit will have succeeded in dulling the erotic charm of their married life. Even if they remain faithful to the promises made in their youth, their spiritual love almost certainly will lose something of its intensity when it is no longer sustained on the physical side. It will usually be sufficient, however, for the purpose of safeguarding the majority of those fundamental goods which marriage has the obligation to insure. Marriage, after all, is not by nature a story of love, but an institution of extreme complexity, in which the social and the individual are inextricably intertwined and cemented by love. Preachers, moralists, educators and writers are wrong in not bringing the complex character of the reality of marriage to light in a better way. They could prevent much disillusionment. Through sublimation, it is always possible for the married lives of a great many men and women to remain sufficiently intimate in character so as not to be considered examples of unhappy marriages. Husbands and wives have to be prepared to replace eroticism by a deep friendship.

Unfortunately for individuals and for the institution of marriage as well, the couples who are capable of a true sublimation are rare. The number is growing of those whom no religious or moral principles forbid to follow the natural inclinations of the flesh. The co-existence of the cult of the body and at the same time a contempt for it is one of the paradoxes of our times. Many men and women are convinced that they are not striking a blow at the deep love which they experience for their wife or husband by yielding to the erotic attraction of another woman or man. They dangerously delude themselves into thinking that they can ignore the intimate solidarity that exists in love between the physical and the spiritual. When sexual relations with the woman who was reputed to be only a temporary mistress turns out to be good, there is every reason to fear that one's heart as well will become attached to her. That will mean the end of a man's "spiritual" love for his wife and the risk of destroying all those individual and social values that are symbolized by the family.

I believe that everything possible should be done to try to sustain eroticism in married life for as long as one can. If it is at all possible, it should play a role right up until the time when nature herself extinguishes the sexual *libido*. "Spiritual couples" themselves would only further their mutual love by prolonging the element of erotic attraction. Such a prolongation is not at all impossible. Reflecting carefully on the analyses of the causes and conditions of the fading and disappearance of eroticism in married life made earlier, each couple ought to be able to discover for itself what ought to be done in their own case to protect it.

8. *Love and the Right of Divorce*

There are those who believe that it is impossible, or that it is detrimental to a person's mental balance, to resist a new erotic attraction. They also consider it utopian to expect that eroticism can be made to last in married life until old age. In all logic, therefore, they favor the right of a husband or a wife to dissolve their marital ties at any time in order to be able to marry someone else.

It is not our task to discuss the many problems of a religious, moral and social nature that are raised by the issue of the right of divorce. Our sole purpose is to investigate the optimal conditions for the furtherance of love. From this standpoint, the psychologist might be tempted at first to take a position against the legal prohibition of divorce. It is not good for husband and wife to feel themselves chained to each other or to enjoy that false security which we have observed to be so often a mortal danger for marital love. In addition, it is well known what a hell life is, in many cases, for two individuals who not only do not understand each other but whose love has gradually turned into hatred. It is also a fact that the legal prohibition of divorce is frequently ineffective even for the purpose of protecting the social values of marriage.

Naturally, the problem is posed in a completely different way for those who believe in the sacramental character of matrimony. They have freely agreed in advance never to divorce each other, no matter what the unforeseen obstacles may be which they are certain to encounter along their way. They are in a position to find in their faith the spiritual energy necessary for choosing the way of sublimation at the time when their love may meet with certain failures on the natural level.

From the psychological point of view, however, the main thing is neither the authorization nor the prohibition of divorce. The only means of saving the institution of matrimony in the present state of personal consciousness is to be concerned with the safeguarding of a total love between husband and wife and with initiating them to the alternative of the various ways of sublimation.

In addition to the religious ideal, it is also possible to conceive that a husband and wife might freely reject divorce on the basis of the sociological value which a stable marriage possesses. The social "mystique" would be sufficiently alive in such a case as to be able to serve as an effective agent of sublimation. But there is no need to insist upon the fact that such cases are very rare in an epoch of heightened individual consciousness.

9. The Cult of Free Love

Of all the contemporary critics of the institution of marriage, Simone de Beauvoir seems to me to come closest to putting a finger on the real problem in The Second Sex. Although she is preoccupied almost exclusively with the question of the liberation of women, our own analyses are not fundamentally different from hers. Men and women in our day do not conceive of marriage except in terms of love; at the same time it is difficult to reconcile marriage and love. On the basis of their own experience, many of them assert that such a reconciliation is existentially impossible. Simone de Beauvoir seems tempted to agree with them.

The psychologist, however, cannot be content with simply observing facts. Without being normative in the same sense that ethics is a normative science, psychology—as I conceive it—is a pragmatic discipline. It certainly does not set out to promote some abstract "good" in itself, but it owes it to itself to make some contribution to the happiness of human life. I feel constrained to point out the fact that neither Simone de Beauvoir nor any other adversary who is against marriage in principle has been able to invent or to suggest any new mode of relationship between men and women that would be free of the evils that beset marriage and at the same time would tend to further the affective expansion and development of the individual in the same degree.

There is, of course, what is called free love (as if it were possible for any love to exist without being free!). With a mixture of astonishment and irony, an example is frequently cited of a pair of lovers who have lived together for years in an atmosphere of the most perfect understanding. Once the obstacles which had been standing in the way of their marriage disappear, they legalize cr regularize their union before a civil authority or a priest. Within the space of a few months, however, the misunderstanding between husband and wife has become so profound that they become divorced!

I have been acquainted with a number of such cases personally, and have been in a position to observe the development of some of them at close range. I have found that it was the apparent security which the state of matrimony confers that caused love to lose that dynamic character which had stimulated the lovers to transcend themselves and to fight against their failings. So long as she was only the mistress of "her man," the woman had made efforts to please him in both a personal and an erotic way. She kept herself dressed in an attractive way and took care to see that her lover would find her beautiful and desirable when he returned home. Almost immediately after their marriage she began to neglect herself. She no longer bothered to hide either her physical defects or the faults of her character. More or less unconsciously, she wanted in this way to affirm her position as a legitimate wife. With her friends in agreement, she said that, after all, "A respectable woman should not desire to seduce her husband the way a young girl wants to seduce a man."

Assuming that a free union is actually more favorable to the element of eroticism than marriage is, would we be correct in considering it as perfectly adapted to the exigencies of love on every other plane as well? My own experience has been that only rare intellectual couples are in a position to expand their personalities fully in such an arrangement. The others inevitably suffer from a feeling of insecurity as well as from the social disapproval which is still usually directed at this sort of liaison. Even if the feeling of the precariousness of the bond does not give way to a feeling of insecurity because of the complete financial independence of each of the partners, and even if society ceases to ostracize individuals who practice free love, would it still not have to be feared that this kind of union might encounter exactly the same obstacles as married life actually encounters? Material security, after all, is not the only thing, nor the principal thing, which love needs.

In the Soviet Union, during the first years following the October Revolution, official favor was bestowed upon free love. Certain prominent feminists like the writer and future ambassadress, Alexandra Kolontaï, had succeeded in linking the cause of the emancipation of women with the cause of the liberation of the proletariat. As we had occasion to note at the beginning of this chapter, they were right in claiming Engels as their authority. He considered marriage to be one of the historical forms of capitalist alienation. In the Soviet Union, therefore, a free union was accorded the same recognition as a legal marriage, it being understood that by degrees, and in proportion to the degree of development of a communist consciousness in the masses, marriage would disappear completely and be replaced by free love. The outcome of this experiment is well known. The suicides of women who had been abandoned took on the proportions of an epidemic. The excessive rate of abortions seriously affected the population of the country and ruined the health of a great number of women; this had disastrous repercussions on the productivity of their labor. In the immense numbers of abandoned infants, vagabonds and criminals, it had to be admitted that the proportion of those who were born of free unions was tragically great. In short, the Soviet Union could not help but recognize the failure of the experiment with free love, from the social point of view. From 1934 on, it has given the same place of honor to the stable, legal family as this holds in the bourgeois society of capitalist countries. It is well known that today Soviet customs in matters concerning love actually veer in the direction of puritanism. Anyone who would still undertake to defend the idea of free love runs a heavy risk of being taken for one of the enemies of the people.

The Soviet experience has also proved that the State cannot be counted upon to relieve women of the cares and fatigue involved in the rearing of their children. It is true—and there is no point in making a secret of it—that these cares frequently put a strain on the love between husband and wife and constitute one of the major obstacles to the development of a free love. But it is also certain that in an agitated world like our own, more now than ever before, if the child is to grow up to become a man worthy of the name, he needs to be surrounded by the affection and security which only his parents are in a position to give him when they themselves have decided never to separate from each other.

10. In Spite of Everything . . .

Our objective in this chapter has been to bring the two existential realities of love and marriage face to face, since they appear to be mutually exclusive. I hope I have not overlooked any of the difficulties which men and women today encounter in marriage, either from the standpoint of their fulfillment as autonomous individuals or from the standpoint of their happiness as a loving couple. I feel constrained to make the point that if it is true that completely successful marriages are not very numerous, nevertheless, up to the present time, no one has been in a position to invent something better than marriage—that is, something which would be favorable to love, eroticism, and the happiness of the children, and which would assume the social function traditionally assigned to the family all at the same time.

The conclusion from all these observations should not be that things should simply be allowed to continue as they have been in the past. In my opinion, there can be no doubt that conservatism—in this area even more than in any other—can only lead to catastrophe and to the erosion of the very values we desire to preserve. Love between a man and a woman, a love that is both spiritual and physical, finds it difficult to realize its tasks of enhancing existence if it pursues its course outside of the security and stability afforded it by marriage. But the traditional forms of conjugal life are more and more found to be out of tune with the present state of human consciousness. A solution has to be found with respect to this antinomy. In marriage, as in political societies and in the Church, there are elements which are permanent and essential, and there are other elements which can justify their existence only in terms of a given state of civilization. It is not by clinging to the transient that the essential can be saved from shipwreck.

In the first place, in the present state of human consciousness (I am speaking, of course, of civilized western man), only marriages of love should be entered into. That does not mean that all that is necessary for marriage is the experience of a fleeting sexual or sentimental emotion. The complexity and seriousness of the psychological reality of love has been insisted upon enough in this book. The education of affectivity has to consist of something infinitely more than simple "sex education." It has to favor the perfect integration of spirit, body, heart and mind.

To insure that only true marriages of love will take place, it is necessary to stop considering marriage as an end in itself. This is especially true for women, many of whom are still inclined to look upon marriage as the most agreeable of all the careers that are offered to them. Because they just want to get married, come what may, they are in an excellent position to engender in themselves and in the other person the illusion of being in love, the unfortunate consequences of which we have had occasion to illustrate by many examples.

In order to prevent marriage from appearing to young girls as the best and easiest path to take, it is important for education to stress that women as much as men should seek self-realization elsewhere, principally in some professional activity. A woman who has a real aptitude for her work and is capable of making a living on her own is much less tempted to want to get married no matter what the cost. She will not marry until she is sure she really is in love. If the majority of women at present are interested in their profession in too superficial a way and are only waiting for the occasion to present itself to have the excuse to abandon it, it is because education and superannuated custom have not made them take it seriously enough. They have been made to look upon it as a temporary occupation. It was not so long ago (and it is still true in some places) that a young girl of the middle class would experience difficulty in admitting that she worked for a living or that she took a real interest in her work. No, she had to be "just occupying her time."

Engaging in the activity of a real profession gives a married woman the economic independence without which it is difficult, if not impossible, to enjoy the moral independence which the modern woman desires so avidly. Even if she has to give up her professional activity in order to attend to her duties as a mother and as the mistress of a household, she presents a psychological picture that is altogether different from the case of a woman who has to be supported by her husband because she is not desirous of, or is incapable of, earning her own living and of acquitting herself of some social function.

Husband and wife also have to be firmly convinced from the very start that even the most passionately genuine love cannot live for very long if it is nourished only by its own substance. Certain precautions have to be taken to prevent the erotic flame from flickering out prematurely. It is important to take care lest the communion of spirits be weakened or destroyed by the banalities of daily life. And like every other love, conjugal love also must be placed at the service of something transcendent. It is only in this way that it will be able to resist triumphantly the attrition of time and habit.

I consider celibacy preferable to a marriage that is based on inauthenticity, a marriage in which there is disharmony between the deeper self and the conditions of the marital arrangement. Modern conditions of life make it possible for those who remain unmarried no longer to resemble the proverbial images of the "old bachelor" and the "old maid."

CHAPTER NINE
CHAIN-LOVE

1. Don Juan

THE CHARACTER of Don Juan, the eternally unsatisfied lover, is an "archetype" in the strict sense of the term as employed by Jung. He symbolizes a psychological experience which, although it certainly is not universal, is nevertheless very widespread. He was made famous by the Spaniard, Tirso de Molina, in the sixteenth century, and by Molière in the seventeenth century. A great number of novelists and playwrights ever since have tried their hand successfully at re-creating his image. Among them were Byron, Lorenzo da Ponte, Goldoni, Alexander Dumas, Prosper Mérimée, Rostand and, quite recently, Henri de Montherlant. There have been other writers who have analyzed the archetype of the chain-lover under different appellations and apparently without having been influenced consciously by the grand tradition. There is a popular Finnish legend, for example, which recounts the gallant adventures of the aristocrat of the South, Don Juan, although the people of the North have probably never even heard his name. Psychological observation confirms the fact that Don Juans are fairly numerous in society.

R. D., a well-educated physician about fifty-five years of age, had been married for almost thirty years. He had never stopped loving his wife. Sexual relations between them were excellent. He looked upon his marriage with complete satisfaction. A short time after the marriage, however, Dr. D. had experienced a sudden, "irresistible" infatuation for one of the nurses who worked with him. He pursued her very assiduously and finally succeeded in making her his mistress. Their liaison lasted for nearly six months. Mrs. D. had been informed of it and suffered a great deal. She could not keep herself from feeling jealous and creating scenes with her unfaithful husband. The latter's separation from his mistress was as sudden, and apparently as little motivated, as his infatuation with her. After a period of strict conjugal fidelity, Dr. D. found the charms of his wife's young maid irresistible. This time

171

again, the flame burned for a few weeks. Then, after several scenes similar to those which had occurred before, it was extinguished, only to flare up again several weeks later with respect to one of his patients.

He carried on in this fashion for almost thirty years. His "conquests" could no longer be counted. In the town in which he practiced, he had the flattering reputation of being a "Don Juan." He tried to make excuses for himself, protesting to his wife that his love for her remained unchanged, and maintaining that he had an "insatiable sexual appetite." The explanation could hardly hold water. At least half of the women whose lover he had been never became his mistress. Frequently, he did not even try to make them so. He was content with letting himself *pass* as their lover. Even in the other cases, his love had a sentimental character more than a sexual one. He felt exhilarated, wrote ardent love letters ("like a sixteen-year-old boy," he said), dedicated poems, made little presents, and so on. It would seem that it was almost by chance that he became a real lover of some of these women. Sometimes it was a case of having to reassure himself of their love for him and establishing stronger ties with the ones who displayed a certain reserve toward him. It was always he who took the initiative in breaking up an affair, and usually when his wife had got wind of it. None of these many loves lasted for more than a year.

The career of a Don Juan is fraught with dramatic events. Several of D.'s mistresses bore him a child. Others of them had abortions. One of them died as a result of the operation, and another committed suicide when she found out he had abandoned her. Mrs. D. evidently did not accept very well the position he placed her in—that of a wife who was perpetually being betrayed. She could not help creating terrible scenes in the house. Several times she was on the point of leaving him. Each time, however, he would cry, fall on his knees, and beg her not to leave him, protesting his undying love, and promising never to do it again. His good resolutions, however, lasted just long enough to allow his wife's wrath to subside.

D. was very conscious, right from the start, of the ephemeral nature of each new amorous adventure. He thought of all the unpleasant things that were in store for him if he succumbed to the attraction he experienced. He was not indifferent either, to the trouble he would again have with his wife. Sometimes he even made laudable efforts to overcome his fascination, but his efforts were rarely crowned with success. Once he undertook the beginning of a fresh conquest, he was convinced that this time it was serious and the really great love of his life. It was not until several months later, after his exalted feeling had dwindled down to zero, that he became conscious again of the pathological character of his passion.

The case of Dr. D. was unusual because of the fact that he loved his wife with a lasting love. It was impossible to doubt his sincerity on this point. Only once had he experienced the desire to leave her in order to "start life over again" with his mistress of the moment, but this desire was of very short duration. Don Juans usually are not capable of forming such deep attachments. They can marry the woman they love at the moment, it is true, but their marital love hardly lasts any longer than their other loves. Some of them divorce, remarry, and divorce again. I knew one man, a fairly well-known lawyer, who was enjoying his seventh marriage, with all six of his former wives still living. Others, whether it is because of the children, or for reasons of social convenience, or even out of simple inertia, stay with their first (or more frequently, their second) wife, while they continue their restless search for love with other women. There are also many Don Juans whose amorous fascination never lasts long enough to induce them to marry.

T. was a high official and a great lover of the plastic arts. At the age of fifty he was still a bachelor, although he was dissatisfied with living alone and had wanted for quite some time to establish a home. He had been in love many times. It was rare for a month to roll by without a new heart-throb for him. He even experienced being drawn by two or three "irresistible attractions" at one and the same time. He pursued the women who set him on fire discreetly but assiduously. He surrounded them with a thousand attentions and gave them presents of books and flowers. He spoke of them with enthusiasm to his friends. In public, at social gatherings, he frequently showed himself so "attentive" that the situation became compromising for the reputation of his lady of the moment. As soon as he was alone with her, however, he immediately reverted to his habitual behavior, which was all discretion and refinement. He was taken—or people pretended to take him—for a great "woman-chaser," and he was proud of his reputation as a conquering Don Juan. In reality, he was forty years old before he became the lover of one of the numerous women he had been in love with. After that, he had had two others as his mistress. But it seems that they, much more than he, saw to that.

As if by chance, T. almost always fell in love with women whom it was impossible for him to marry and whose lover he could hope to become only with great difficulty. For a long time he was interested only in married women whose reputation was above reproach and preferably ones who were known to possess ardent religious convictions. Although he considered himself an atheist and totally amoral, and although he was forty years old at the time, T. had been greatly shocked when one of these virtuous and pious women freely offered herself to him instead of resisting his attentions. The liaison lasted for only a few weeks; the disappointment of T. had been so great that his love vanished as if by enchantment.

In spite of the fact that he did not really consider himself young any more, T. could experience sudden infatuation only for virgins who were under twenty. He was too prudent to marry so young a person, and too honest and good (he told himself) to make them unhappy by being the means of their losing their virginity. He therefore established himself in the role of being a "platonic" Don Juan.

Not every Don Juan, obviously, is so scrupulous as T. was. S. was a celebrated writer very much appreciated in Catholic circles because of his sublime ideas on love. Like T., he could fall in love only with virgins or with married women of untarnished morality. He could not rest, however, until he persuaded the faithful wife to renounce for him the fidelity to her husband which she had sworn to before God, and until he persuaded the chaste virgin to make him a present of her virtue. When he ceased to be in love with them (which did not take him very long) he would have acquired enough spiritual domination over them to make them return to being the same virtuous and chaste women they had been before they had had relations with him. Knowing how completely illogical it was, he was personally convinced that these wives and virgins had done nothing reprehensible in giving themselves to him, but that they would be conducting themselves in an unworthy and immoral manner if they took up with another lover. He directed several of his former mistresses to enter a convent. But most of them did not stay there very long. Whenever he learned that a married woman who had been his mistress was now the mistress of another man and was contemplating divorce, he would write her one "mystical" letter after another, trying to dissuade her from sin. If he did not succeed by this method, he set about making her his own mistress again in the hope of thus preventing her from "straying from the straight and narrow path." He was perfectly sincere in his books, in which he extolled virtue in general and the virtue of chastity in particular.

There are many Don Juans in the world. I have expressly chosen Dr. D., the high official, T., and the writer, S., as examples to shed some light on the psychology of a Don Juan. All three of them were men of the better sort. None of them would be mistaken for a vulgar rake who was looking for nothing more than one new sexual pleasure after another. The three men whose cases we have presented were men of refined sensibilities. On each occasion of their sudden infatuations, the primacy of sentiment or feeling over anything else was unquestionable. T., for example, usually sought sexual pleasure outside the area of his amorous experiences. As the majority of the great writers who have dealt with this theme have understood and made plain, the true Don Juan is infinitely more hungry for love than thirsty for pleasure. He is still a "romantic" at an age when other men are already so perfectly adjusted to reality that they recall the ardors of their youth with only a tender and ironic smile. In spite of appearances to the contrary, a Don Juan is almost always a man who has not yet overcome certain psychological conflicts of his adolescence or of his childhood.

As an adolescent, D. had no desire whatsoever to become a physician. He had a most fervent desire to

become a missionary-priest. His father was an unbeliever
and categorically opposed to the idea. It seemed incomprehensible to him in a boy who was so talented and so
full of life. Out of sheer inertia, and because he did not
experience a positive attraction for any secular career, D.
succumbed to his mother's entreaties and went to medical
school. As frequently happens with individuals who are
seeking the Absolute and who are prevented from following their own path, D. repressed all of his religious feeling
in order not to feel pain at the loss of his vocation. He
married for love and never ceased loving his wife. But the
love of a woman was not sufficient to satisfy emotionally
an existence in which the exercise of a profession was
only a means of making a livelihood, and consequently a
burden. The numerous infatuations Dr. D. experienced
seem to be explainable in terms of the emptiness in his
heart and the unconscious quest for an affective fulfillment which no human love was in a position to give him.
It reminds me of the parable in the Gospel about the
house from which the demon was expelled and which
was swept clean. Because it was left empty, the demon
returned with seven other demons worse than himself. In
reality, D. was not looking for the kind of affection and
pleasure which women were able to give him to a certain
extent. For him, they were only substitutes for another
love, one for which his unconscious had never ceased to
experience a thirst. Why be astonished that he could not
remain attached to any of them for any length of time,
when none of them was the Absolute? To cure D. of
being a Don Juan—which had become in him a real
neurosis—he would have to be helped to discover in his
existence an exalted positive meaning, an ideal that would
be equal, subjectively, to the missionary ideal of his youth.

The mother of Mr. T., the almost platonic Don Juan,
had been abandoned very early by her husband, when
her son was still a baby. As frequently happens in such
situations, she concentrated all her frustrated need for
affection on her child. It was for his sake that she always
had refused to remarry. In order for him to be able to go
to school and to grow up to be a "gentleman," she had
worked very hard for many years. But—and this is also
common in such situations—she expected in return for all
this that her child, and later the young man, would love

no one but herself. She forbade him to have any friends on the excuse of keeping him away from bad example. She expected him to spend all of his free time in her company. She succeeded in inspiring in him at a very early age a real horror for women. Apparently forgetting that she was a woman herself, she identified all women with that "most despicable of creatures" who was the cause of her husband's leaving her and her child. The little boy formed for himself an idea of the fair sex as resembling an impure demon. During his school years T. instinctively had fled the company of young girls. He displayed a discouraging timidity in their presence. His mother died a short time after he passed his examination for the post of inspector of finance. He remained in mourning for several years and experienced a sense of absolute abandonment. Gradually, as his grief began to diminish, the desire grew in him to marry and to establish with another woman a relationship of profound spiritual intimacy like the one he had known with his mother. He was naturally attracted by respectable women, who were in this respect similar to his mother. But the fear of women which his mother had instilled in him always lay hidden in his unconscious. That is why he always fell in love with women whom it was impossible for him to marry. In order for him to become capable of forming an attachment, and no longer to idealize a woman in terms of the image of his mother, or to despise her as her rival, Mr. T. had to be liberated from the posthumous domination of his mother.

S., the writer, had known a childhood and an adolescence completely devoid of love. His mother had been a very worldly woman. She paid hardly any attention to her son, leaving him to be cared for by the servants. He was only ten years old when he surprised her in the arms of one of her lovers. He conceived a violent hatred for her which was to extend itself to all women, especially since there were several others in the family household who were hardly less frivolous than his mother. At a very young age, S. became a passionate reader of sentimental love stories. In them he found a way of escaping from his real world, which was emotionally so empty, into an atmosphere of purity and noble sentiments. As an adolescent he amused himself by dreaming for hours that he was in love with a young girl who was as beautiful and pure as the heroines in the books he read. When one day he saw a young girl who was the momentary object of his affection go off to the bathroom, he received such a rude shock that it immediately put an end to his love. He knew very well that even princesses were not exempt from physiological necessities, but everything which bore a relation to the body and its needs seemed to him so ugly and shameful that he categorically refused to allow himself to think about it. And in the stories which he loved there was never any question of anyone having to go to the bathroom or of having to take a bath. Even meals were taken more in the spirit of a ceremony than as a means of satisfying bodily needs. His own first novels were just as "pure." That is undoubtedly the reason he obtained such a quick success in respectable circles.

He had his first mistress at the age of twenty-two. He suffered a bitter disappointment when he discovered that she had not been a virgin before she had relations with him. The liaison did not last. But it was from that time on that S. became a chaser and a seducer of young girls who were virgins. Later on he discovered that he had just as strong an inclination toward wives who were good women and faithful to their husbands. He experienced an imperious need to feel that he was the lover of women who were as different as possible from his flighty mother, and that in turn he was loved by them. He could not think of his mother without experiencing contempt for her. He so much wanted to respect their purity and virtue, which he extolled in his novels. But unless he could get the woman or the young girl whom he admired and loved to sacrifice her virtue to him, he felt terribly uneasy because he could not believe in her love. In giving herself to him, however, she ceased to be a virgin or a faithful wife, and he could no longer admire her. The fire of his love would then quickly flicker out. He would then play the good apostle again, using all his prestige to get the one he had seduced to become chaste again or to become once more a faithful wife. Sometimes he succeeded and this heightened his self-esteem a great deal, for he had the happy faculty of forgetting that he himself had been the seducer. On the other hand, when he learned that one of his former mistresses had taken a new lover, he was sincerely pained by it. This was certainly a case of jealousy. His unconscious experienced it as an insult and a humiliation that he was not the only man who was capable of turning a good woman away from the path of righteousness. In spite of his success as a writer and as a man of the world, he still had not been able to free himself from the feeling of inferiority which had resulted from the emotional frustration that had marred his childhood. It was in order to compensate for it that he felt the need to assure himself of the love of so many "good" women. But if these very women were susceptible of experiencing a similar passion for other men, how then could S. continue to believe in his own superiority?

But S. was also tortured by a feeling of guilt. He told himself (not without a certain complacency) that if he had not seduced her the first time and had not given her a taste for the forbidden fruit, this young girl would still be a virgin and this woman a faithful wife. But he was satisfied that neither was in any danger of allowing themselves to be deflected from the right path by some "vulgar seducer." When it was a question of himself, our novelist—like all narcissists—found a thousand excuses for women to prefer him to their moral and religious principles. On the other hand, as soon as there was a question of another man, he again became the strict moralist his novels had given him the reputation of being.

The seduction of a very young girl who was a virgin created a scandal which threatened to compromise S.'s career as a respectable writer. It was then he determined to seek psychological help. Little by little, he had to become reconciled toward his mother, and his inferiority complex had to be overcome. He set himself to writing novels in which love and women were no longer idealized in an exaggerated way. When he fell in love again with a young girl he did not experience any desire to reassure himself about the intensity of her feelings by making her his mistress. He married her. And it seems that this put a definite end to his career as a Don Juan.

2. *Messalina*

There were two Roman matrons, each with the name

of Messalina. One was the wife of the Emperor Claudius and the other was the third wife of Nero. Both have become famous because of their love affairs and debauchery. It is always a dangerous undertaking to attempt to psychoanalyze persons who have long since died and about whom we know very little. Freud, himself, however, applied the principles of psychoanalysis to a study of Leonardo da Vinci. René Laforgue did the same thing in the case of Talleyrand, and other psychoanalysts have "analyzed" a number of historical personages. It should be well understood that such analysis cannot claim conclusions of a truly scientific character. The essential factor in the method of psychoanalysis—free association—could not possibly play any role. It remains true, nevertheless, that it is possible to draw many interesting lessons from an interpretation of the works and the known behavior of a historical personage if it is based on those principles of psychoanalysis that can be deemed certain.

For my own part, I have no desire to explain the amorous conduct of the two matrons in question in terms of psychosynthesis. We know too little about them. But like many other depth psychologists, I consider the name Messalina a convenient symbol to denote the feminine counterpart of Don Juan. One could just as well speak about Catherine the Great of Russia, whose love life was just as tumultuous as that of the two Roman women by the name of Messalina. And if we want to employ a famous symbol to signify the platonic form of "Messalinism," Elizabeth I of England might be chosen.

Call them what you will, Messalinas, Catherines, or Elizabeths, it is unquestionable that the women who have one love after another are just as numerous as are the imitators of Don Juan.

Agnes came from a wealthy, aristocratic family. In contradiction to the principles which were held most sacred in her circle of society, she had had her first lover when she was only eighteen years of age. Her seducer—if he can really be called that, since the young girl's own curiosity was the true instigator—was a casual companion she had met while on vacation. The liaison ended when the vacation was over. When the young man tried to speak about marriage, Agnes's only response was always a silly, ironic kind of laughter. For five years then

Agnes carried on in a sort of frenzy with one lover after another. She became an object of scandal for her family. She astonished even her friends and acquaintances, although their own morals were very loose. Her heart and her senses became inflamed with equal readiness. The flame would then flicker out just as suddenly. Young boys and mature men succeeded one another on her list of pursued lovers.

When she was twenty-three years old, Agnes fell in love with a man of high social position appreciably older than herself. Although she had been categorically refusing all offers of marriage until then, this time she married her lover. She sincerely desired to remain faithful to him, and for two years she succeeded perfectly. Then the demon took over again, and she began a new chain of sentimental and erotic adventures.

It would be a mistake to view this twentieth-century Messalina as a gross sensualist. Quite the reverse is true. She never experienced an orgasm in the arms of any of the men who had intercourse with her. The thing that will surprise the layman the most is the fact that (because of the puritanical education she had received) this libertine retained a strong aversion for sex in general and for her own body in particular. She found sexual intercourse "disgusting." Each time she had intercourse, she experienced a sensation of being soiled. She was no sooner out of the arms of her lover or husband than she would wash and scrub herself with a desperate kind of thoroughness. The emotional pleasure which she derived from her many amours was not very satisfying either. As soon as she had "had" a man, she would treat him as a "low cad," a common pleasure-seeker, incapable of appreciating the high esthetic level on which her own love existed.

Agnes's husband learned of her repeated infidelities, and he threatened to divorce her. Having read a popular work on psychoanalysis, the young woman thought that there might very well be something pathological about her behavior and about the impossibility of her being satisfied emotionally by being faithful to one man. She went to see a psychotherapist. He maintained that it was precisely her radical frigidity that had made Agnes into a Messalina.

With the education which she had received, Agnes would never have dared think that she might love a man other than her husband, and with all the more reason, that she might ever give herself to another man. From the time of her adolescence, she was very curious about sexual matters, but there was no sensuality involved in her curiosity. It was out of curiosity, a curiosity which, I would say, was strictly of an intellectual nature, that she gave herself to a man for the first time. Under these conditions her lover could only disappoint her, and she retained a very disagreeable memory of her deflowering. The feeling of having committed an irreparable moral fault was added to the physical pain she experienced. She had been—or thought she had been—in love with the young man before the event. After it, she no longer had any affection whatsoever for him. But she continued to have relations with him for several weeks because she felt she had nothing more to lose, and because she had an unconscious desire to punish herself for her first fault. It would have been a psychological miracle if, in such a state of mind, she had been able to find any pleasure in love.

Agnes was young. The education she had received reinforced her tendencies toward idealism and romanticism. As painful as her first disappointment had been, it had not killed in her all hope of encountering the "grand amour" or the desire to experience the joys of love. Every time a man pleased her and seemed to be interested in her, she was seized with a strange panic which was a mixture of hope for success and fear of a new failure. Failure and disappointment naturally kept repeating themselves.

The original cause of Agnes's erotic and emotional instability, the cause of her frigidity, went back to a time prior to her first amorous experience. She had suffered a serious trauma in adolescence. She said she had completely forgotten that when she was twelve years old, a man on the crowded subway-train had tried to fondle her in a "disgusting" way. She experienced a violent psychological shock which was an unconscious factor in Agnes's emotional impoverishment. She finally became capable of fidelity and of experiencing pleasure when the initial trauma and its sequelae were liquidated.

Is every Messalina as frigid as Agnes was? It would be hazardous to make any categorical statement about a matter which does not lend itself to statistical analysis very well. The observations made by several other psychoanalysts and psychologists, however, perfectly confirm what I myself have been able to find out from the study of certain cases which I was in a position to follow very closely. In his remarkable book, *Frigidity in Woman in Relation to Her Love Life,* Stekel devoted a long chapter to a very detailed exposition of the case of a Messalina. The celebrated psychoanalyst declares that Messalinas "have had innumerable liaisons, but have always been insensible during them. . . . They are seekers of love, but they do not find its fulfillment." As in the case of Agnes, so in the Messalinas encountered by Stekel: the inability to find joy and pleasure in love is not a physiological deficiency but a neurosis, a true sickness of the soul. Like Don Juan, Messalina is almost always a neurotic individual. It is the *superego,* the strength of which is particularly great in the psychic apparatus of such emotionally sick persons, which prohibits them from experiencing the happiness of love and thus renders every amorous experience disappointing. Guilt is the dominant factor that is most frequently encountered in such a rigid and severe *superego.* As much as they hope finally to experience pleasure, it is the unconscious desire to expiate sin through suffering which pushes Messalinas toward one disappointing experience after another. To cure them, it is necessary to get their conscience, which has been under the sway of their *superego,* no longer to prohibit them from experiencing pleasure, or from no longer imposing the self-punishment on them of depriving themselves of the experience of having an orgasm.

I encountered one Messalina, however, in whom the dominant factor was her rejection of femininity. Only the masculine way of making love seemed noble to her. As a woman she felt herself humiliated by having passively to depend upon her partner for her pleasure. She therefore forbade herself to experience an orgasm which, in her mind, would have meant handing herself over to a man's superiority. The emotional dissatisfaction resulting from this "hardening" carried her unceasingly from one amorous adventure to another, from which her unconscious hoped finally to derive the joy she was rejecting. The remedy in such a case lies in reconciling a woman to her own femininity. A man will then no longer appear to her as a rival against whom she has to keep up the fight, but as a partner with whom she can communicate.

CHAPTER TEN

THE DEATH OF LOVE

IT IS of the essence of all true love to believe in its own immortality. It is the existential act *par excellence*. It activates simultaneously both body and soul. It totally engulfs our "heart." How, therefore, can we avoid believing and hoping that it will endure for as long as existence itself? Persons who believe in an eternal life would find it less attractive if they could not hope to discover in the next world those whom they have loved on earth, and with whom they can expect to renew their former emotional ties. It is true that the Christian paradise, unlike that of the Moslem, does not promise men sensual joys; but Christians hold that once they have entered heaven their spiritualization will have been so developed as to enable them to be happy with the joys of a purely spiritual love. In short, a person in love is almost always sincere when he vows "eternal love" to his beloved, even when he or she is not the first one to whom he has done so.

After all that one has either personally experienced, or at least seen and heard, one is inclined to conclude that in practice, unfortunately, immortal love can be found only in the old Russian novels. Nearly all the husbands and wives in the divorce courts, who hurl words of reproach and hatred at each other, at one time in the past had vowed eternal love for each other, and sometimes not too long before. The young wife who was brought before the tribunal of justice for having killed her husband, a minister of State, had also once entered into a marriage of love. The same thing can be said about those wives who slowly poison their husbands with arsenic, or those husbands who display a vicious ingenuity in the way they get rid of their wives. It is amazing, and quite disconcerting, how, in the face of all this, men and women can go on believing in the permanent character of their love.

Marguerite had a falling out with her parents and cheerfully renounced a large inheritance in order to marry the man without whom, she thought, life would not be worth living. The fact that he was poor and did not belong to her social class at all only made her esteem him the more highly. She interpreted this fact as an additional proof of the genuineness and undying character of her passion. It lasted for ten years. Marguerite then suddenly realized that she loved another man with "eternal love" again, and that she now experienced only disgust and annoyance with her husband. She could not understand at all how she could have thought she ever loved him and how she could have left both her parents and her fortune for him. She reproached him as having been the cause of her wasting her life. Being assured her new love desired her, she left her husband without the slightest regret "in order to remake her life." She even took from him the little money they had managed to save through countless sacrifices during the course of the ten years in which they had lived together.

James, a small-town school teacher, was almost as patient as his namesake Jacob in the Old Testament. He wanted to marry a woman without whom he was certain he could not go on living. Unfortunately, she was another man's wife, and James had to wait several years before her husband would give his consent to a divorce. Meanwhile James had to put up with all sorts of humiliating situations. He became the object of his students' gibes, and they wrote things about him on the walls. When at last he was able to marry his beloved, he had to break his ties with the religious community of which he had been a devout member, since it did not approve of marriage with a divorcée. A cultivated man with refined feelings ordinarily, in the face of what seemed to him to be "malicious obstinacy" on the part of the husband, James for a moment got to the point of entertaining the thought of killing him—perhaps by means of a well-planned automobile accident. Not knowing how it could be done, and also profiting from a moment of clarity, James never committed the crime; but the fact that a man like himself would have even thought of such a thing made it even more undeniable in his eyes that his love was of a very exceptional character. In his personal diary, he compared himself to Abraham, whom Yahweh commanded to sacrifice his only son Isaac. However, after several months of married life with the woman whom he had loved so long with an "eternal love," James suddenly realized to his sorrow and amazement that he did not love her any more.

He held it terribly much against his wife that he had gone through so much commotion in his life just to be able to marry her. From being a man who was very gentle, he became hateful and violent. He made his wife's life so unbearable by his temper and by physical blows that in a panic of despair she committed suicide. As for James, he then went completely to seed.

It may appear surprising that a violent love should die suddenly or that it should be transformed into equally violent hatred. Actually, however, there is nothing sudden in this process, except the conscious realization of it. In the case of Marguerite, love exhausted itself slowly in the battle against the restraints of a mediocre way of life, very different from what she had been accustomed to. Once love died, it became more difficult to put up with these restraints. When she fell in love with another man, she saw in her husband only an obstacle to her love, so much so that she hated him. In James's case also, love did not turn to hate all of a sudden. The flame of love had been extinguished even before the woman had obtained her divorce. But he had suffered and fought so long in the name of this love! It is not surprising that he refused to recognize its death: he would have been constrained to admit that he had suffered and fought for nothing. So he continued to play the game, as much for himself as for others. It was because he did not love her any more that it was only a short time after he had married her that he came to the sad realization of all that the desire for possession of this woman had cost him, both materially and morally. In his case too, hate made its appearance only at a second stage—namely, when he no longer experienced anything except the drawbacks involved in their union.

It is only in rare instances, however, that the place left vacant by the death of love is occupied by hate. It is an axiom dear to psychologists that the contrary of love is not hatred but indifference. This axiom can be verified in the majority of cases. Indifference nibbles away at even the most balanced kind of love, the kind that is most in accord with the laws of both God and man. It is not easy to keep love from being consumed by the wear and tear of time, especially since almost no one in love has any idea of how necessary it is to do something to safeguard what appears to them to be something of a purely spontaneous nature. Besides, many people—and particularly women—refuse with all their might to admit to the death of a love which they have believed and desired to be eternal. It is as if to recognize that they are no longer in love means that they are obliged to deny their entire past and to avow that they have deceived themselves into believing they were in love when they were not, and thus had built their life on an illusion. Unfortunately, this refusal to recognize the true state of affairs is insufficient to enable these persons to behave with the generosity which befits love. If it were possible for them to exhibit such generosity, one would be tempted to congratulate them on their ability to live on illusion. But it is sufficient to observe their behavior to realize their lack of love.

Madame F. had been married in the dazzling glow of youthful love. For several years, however, she had been neglecting her husband. She took less and less good care of his laundry and clothing. She did not bother any more to cook the dishes that he liked. Sexual relations had become a tiresome duty to her, and she seized on the slightest pretext to be able to forego them. But she was persuaded that she still loved her husband as much as she did the first day they were married. She wrote him endearing letters when he was away. Even with her most intimate friends she insisted on her unalterable love. Finding her joy in living fading more and more, Madame F. decided to see a psychotherapist. In the course of treatment it came to light that she had stopped loving her husband a long time ago, and that her "great love" was dead without any hope of its being resurrected. Her unconscious had refused to admit that she had deceived herself in marrying this man, with whom she had nothing in common of a profound nature. She also wanted her children to have "normal" parents. She therefore obstinately clung to the illusion of an eternal love. The irritableness of her character, her laziness, her passivity, and finally her loss of all joy in living were the consequence of the exhausting battle she was waging in order to safeguard her illusion.

Many men and women do not believe in love at all either because they have personally experienced its death or because they have observed it die in others. They consciously subscribe to pessimistic theories, according to which love is only an illusion, a trick, a travesty of the sexual instinct in those who want at all costs to consider themselves different from the animals. They logically conclude that, this being the case, it is preferable to reject love in all clarity rather than become involved in the eventual suffering such an illusion will inevitably entail. The apostles of this doctrine think they will no longer be exposed to any anxiety, disillusionment, or heartbreak if they no longer speak of love, but simply let themselves be guided by instinct, fully conscious of its ephemeral nature. The "return to nature" is the great remedy against neurosis!

The "existentialism" which not so long ago was all the rage in the "caves" of Saint-Germain-des-Pres, is not the only movement propounding this thesis. A fairly large number of sexologists and psychoanalysts, who consider themselves the orthodox disciples of Freud, are of the opinion that there is nothing "real" in love except sexual instinct. It goes without saying, of course, that for them every instinct is by nature an exclusively biological concern. In the final analysis, love is a neurotic phenomenon engendered by the *superego,* and the source of painful conflicts.

One might be tempted to acknowledge a pragmatic justification of this conception of love if it could be proved that the blasé individuals who refuse to believe in genuine love succeeded in experiencing an affective development which was better than those whose ambition is to experience a mortal love with the fervor of an immortal passion. Experience constrains us, however, to declare the opposite. The man and woman who have loved each other with an ardent love have been given an existential enrichment which will last even when love shall have lost its ardor or even have died completely. On the other hand, those who have sought from each other only passing pleasure, the simple satisfaction of instinctive impulse, will infallibly experience emptiness and nothingness since the possibility or the desire for joy will be missing.

This is not said in defense of illusion. Amorous autosuggestion is not being suggested here on the excuse of putting one's self in the position of finding a greater affective development than in the "truth of instinct." Anything founded on a lie cannot be anything but illusory. Mortal or not, it is love that is *true*. It is real, just as real as our earthly life itself, which is likewise mortal. Even those who do not believe in an eternal life generally find this life sufficiently beautiful and interesting to go on living in spite of all the sorrows and sufferings that come their way. Why would the situation not be the same in the case of love?

Neither psychological nor ordinary observation authorize us, however, to consider it inevitable that love between a man and a woman will be transformed into hatred or indifference. There are countless couples in whose case it is impossible to speak about hate or indifference after a long life together. The two partners remain in love with each other, sometimes more so than on the first day of their marriage, although in a different way.

It is undoubtedly difficult, if not impossible psychologically, to rekindle the flames of a love that is dead. The resurrection of the dead always requires a miracle. On the other hand, hygiene and medicine are often in a position to prevent death from occurring prematurely. In the same way, it is also possible to prevent love from dying.

The first precaution to be taken by those who desire a love that will be "immortal" is that they not believe that the moon is made of green cheese: that is to say, that they should not mistake for love what may simply be sensual attraction—or worse (as we have observed it can be in certain cases) a neurotic fixation. It must be remembered that in all genuine love the carnal and the spiritual have to be harmonized as much as possible.

Sexual passion by itself, even "poeticized," is altogether inadequate to serve as a support for an existential communion one desires should last. It is its nature, as we have seen, to lose its intensity by degrees and finally to become extinguished. It is equally natural and easy for an instinct to exchange one object for another. Besides, the different ailments that are inevitably attendant upon old age will one day put an end to purely carnal love. The sequel to carnal passion, moreover, is very frequently indifference, and sometimes hatred.

A love that is purely spiritual, growing as it does out of deep affinities of an ethical, esthetic, intellectual and religious nature, is more durable than passion. There have been a number of famous couples in history in whose union sexual attraction seems to have played almost no role, and whose love nevertheless victoriously resisted the wear and tear of time. I am thinking of Lenin and Kroupskaia, of Louis the Fourteenth and Madame de Maintenon, and many others. It is true that such situations and such persons are exceptional. In ordinary life, a love that is purely spiritual is far from being exempt from stumbling blocks. It cannot be considered the normal thing except at the end of a long, progressive process of spiritualization, but almost never at the beginning.

It is not at all exceptional, however, for a love to die, even though it may have been born under the best auspices of a harmony between the spiritual and the physical.

Madame P. was completely upset about what was happening to her. She and her husband were so much in love with each other. They shared the same ideas and the same aspirations, and they understood each other in bed perfectly at the same time. They loved each other so much that they were sufficient unto themselves and felt the need for no one else. Even the arrival of a baby would have seemed an interference. The money which they earned they spent on pleasures they enjoyed together. They had champagne-suppers alone together and went on luxurious vacation trips. They dreamed of living together in their old age, in some idyllic spot and with great comfort. But suddenly, even before their middle age, her husband left her for another woman, telling her that for a long time he "did not feel anything" for her. What had Madame P. all the more at sea was the fact that she herself was not so certain she always loved her husband.

The depth psychologist had no difficulty at all in

explaining the death of such a love. Love is not in a position to nourish itself on its own substance alone. Its very essence is generosity; it is dynamic and creative. As perfect as one may suppose it to be in the beginning, it is essential for it to grow and to be productive. Egoism *à deux* is as mortal an enemy to it as solitary selfishness. Lovers who yield to the temptation which lies in wait for them to turn in on themselves, to cut themselves off from the external world, by degrees arrive at the point where they have nothing to say to each other. Interesting subjects of conversation are exhausted quickly in a closet. Communion of minds can die of inanition for want of renewed nourishment.

In order to insure that love will last as long as possible, it is indispensable that each couple in its own way (and each member of the couple in his and her own way) never give up trying to develop the richness of their own personality. It is best when the two partners are bound together in the service of a single ideal, whether it be art, social justice or, preferably, God. According to the celebrated postulate of Karl Jaspers, there can be no authentic individual existence without an intrinsic reference to the Transcendent. In the same way, a love which cements the existence of a couple has equally to be integrated into a Love which transcends the couple. The only person who truly lives is the one who acknowledges that something exists for which he would be ready to sacrifice his life. In the same way, a love which does not acknowledge anything which merits its being sacrificed for, does not give any promise of being of a truly lasting nature.

It would be a serious psychological error, however, not to attend to the matter of a constant renewal of a communion of minds. Love between a man and a woman is by definition something very different from a sublime friendship. It is true, as we saw before, that it is difficult, if not impossible, to prevent the erotic attraction from being in jeopardy. Old age infallibly will put an end to it. Still, it is essential not to let it die prematurely. In the chapter devoted to marriage, I have indicated certain precautions that can be taken to prevent routine from killing sensual love. Proof that it is possible to insure, if not immortality, at least an appreciably longer life for it than it ordinarily has, is furnished by those married couples and lovers who still experience a mutual erotic attraction for each other even after thirty or forty years of living together. It is important to realize, however, that all the couples of this type which I have known are couples whose communion of spirits is one of great intensity.

The essential thing to do, therefore, to prevent love from gradually dying, is to attend to the matter of intensifying love on the psychological plane right from the start. This must help to compensate to the maximum for the usually inevitable diminution of sexual love. One may call this sublimation if he wants to, but this sort of sublimation has very little in common with the unconscious mechanisms designated as sublimation in Freudian psychoanalytic vocabulary.

CHAPTER ELEVEN

THE LOVE OF FRIENDSHIP

IN THE course of the preceding chapters of this book, I have frequently departed from the use of Freudian conceptions. The reasons for doing so were not of a religious or moral nature at all; they were exclusively psychological reasons. Together with Jung and many other noted psychologists, I think that the basic principle of the Freudian theory of love is contradicted by psychological experience. For Freudian psychoanalysis, affective energy—the *libido* —is sexual in nature. It follows from this that every time affectivity is manifested in a form which is not sexual in character it has to be spoken about in terms of either a deviation or a sublimation, the latter term being understood in the pejorative sense which signifies something unauthentic. As a result of this, a friendship between two persons of the same sex would have to be considered an example of disguised homosexuality. A friendship between two persons of the opposite sex would be related to a sublimation, more or less in good faith, of sexual desire.

I have pointed out elsewhere the weak points and the ambiguities which the Freudian theory of the *libido* contains. The founder of psychoanalysis generally speaks of the *libido* as the equivalent of the sexual impulse. His extension of it to other domains of affective life clearly constitutes an abuse. Sometimes, however, it is true that in the writings of Freud *libido* means affective energy in its totality. It is impossible in that case to see what right any one has to consider its sexual expression as the prototype of all its activities.

1. *Metamorphoses of the* Libido

Every depth psychologist shares the personal conviction (based upon his experience) that a certain relationship exists among all the forms of affective life. Nothing, however, authorizes us to consider one of them—the sexual form, let us say—as being the only one that is authentic, and of which all the others are so many more or less worthy deviations.

Affective energy—which one rightly can call *libido*—undoubtedly is one form. It is absolutely undifferentiated in itself, however. It acquires a determinate coloring only from the end toward which it is being employed. The same psychic energy nourishes the erotic love between a man and a woman, filial, paternal and fraternal love, the love of science, of art, of philosophy, friendship, and even the mystical love of God.

No one of these different types of love enjoys any natural privilege over the others. To say, for example, that friendship is a more or less successful counterfeit of erotic love is no more justifiable than to say that the attraction which a man experiences for a woman is a deviation from his passion for beautiful landscapes.

On the other hand, it is unquestionable that no matter what the affective activity may be, when it is very intense it is likely to consume such a great amount of energy, or *libido,* that there is hardly anything of it left to be put at the disposition of the other psychic dynamisms. A child who is too passionately attached to his parents, for example, will refuse to love his brothers and sisters. Instead, he will be tempted to look upon them as rivals. He will not be open any more to forming friendships, and if while he is growing up he does not succeed in normalizing his emotional relations with his parents, he will not be capable any more, as an adult, of experiencing erotic love. It is a well known fact that there are certain men of science who are too passionately interested in their research to have the slightest interest in anything which seems to them foreign to their own specialty, whether it be a wife, their children, or anything else. Erotic love, even more than the other forms of love, is capable of such an intense consumption of energy that there can be nothing left for friendship, or even for the love of one's parents. Who does not know cases of lovers "under a spell" who live only for each other, so much so that they are even jealous of their own children? There is reason to rejoice that the flame of erotic love generally possesses an ephemeral character. In the case of normal lovers, the feeling remains intense for only a short while. It becomes normal-ized quickly enough to permit them again to love other things and other persons at the same time as they go on loving each other.

The more normal individual, one who is endowed with a normal degree of affective energy, can utilize this affec-tive energy simultaneously in the direction of all sorts of love—erotic love and friendship, family affection, passion for study, and so on. As a general rule, however, even in the most normal individuals one form of love predom-inates. In the majority of cases, the *libido* is utilized most intensely now in one, now in another domain at different successive or alternating stages. In the case of children, it is naturally the love of parents which occupies the dominant position. This normally is succeeded in adolescence by a preference shown to friends. In young people, erotic love alternates—not without difficulty—with the love of art or of study, and there are sometimes regressions to an older form of love that one might have thought had been definitively superseded. In the normal adult, however, enough energy remains available to pre-vent those affections which momentarily appear to be of lesser importance to him from becoming atrophied for lack of nourishment. A man can certainly love a woman with a passion which, for the moment, seems to deprive everything else of its importance. He continues, however, to love his parents and his friends no less, and his profession as well.

2. The Furtherance of Existence through Friendship

The role of friendship in the affective expansion and development of human beings—and thus in the success-fulness of their lives—is a primary one. The man who has never had any friends has more to complain about perhaps than the man who has never loved or been loved. In the case of young people, it is generally by means of friendship that their necessary extroversion, their branching out into the external world, is accomplished. Mother, father, brothers and sisters, who are always the first objects of love for the child, are too close for him to experience them as really belonging to the outer world. As long as love is still only familial, it remains narcissistic.

The individual who loves only his own family will be a fatal misfit in life. More often than not he will wind up at the psychiatric clinic. When a child at kindergarten or grammar school makes his first friend, he experiences an exhilarating joy and a great pride. He has the impression of having been singled out and chosen personally, and therefore of having become an independent individual.

Individuals who are neurotically attached to their parents and to the family circle in general, reject the opportunity of opening out to the external world which friendship provides them. Either they avoid the slightest intimate relationship with others, or they behave in such a way toward them that they only discourage any friendly overtures. A more subtle and more ambivalent way of rejecting friendship because it would act as a means of turning one toward the outside world, consists in wanting to integrate one's friend within the family and to create a bond with him which is identical with the bond which unites brothers and sisters or parents and children.

Laura, one of the daughters of a large family, at twenty-five was still very much attached to all of the members of her family. She did not dare do anything, or even feel or think about anything, without first being assured of her mother's approval. She idealized her parents to an exaggerated degree, refusing to recognize even the slightest fault in them. She always referred to their authority in discussions with her friends at school. She took upon herself an enormous number of obligations and responsibilities with regard to her brothers and sisters. Using the excuse that they were unhappy, she frequently sacrificed her own chances for happiness and for having a "good time." Laura did not display any aversion to friendship. At high school and college she had formed close ties with some of her comrades, and the other students thought she was "a swell girl." She considered it to be absolutely necessary, however, for all of her friends to become integrated within her family. She more or less consciously engineered them into engagements with one or another of her brothers, and she reacted badly to the engagement of one of her brothers with a young girl who was not one of her own friends.

The Freudians undoubtedly would maintain that Laura experienced an unconscious incestuous love for her brothers; her *superego* naturally forbade her to commit incest, so she was searching for a way to love her brothers through her friends, with whom she identified herself. Such an interpretation rests upon the classical Freudian identification of affectivity in its entirety with sexuality, an identification which we have seen is one that cannot be justified in the light of psychological experience. Not that such cases of incest by proxy are absolutely inconceivable. Such cases undoubtedly exist. That does not authorize us, however, to use them as the basis for constructing a principle of explanation to cover all cases.

I knew Laura very well. I think I can furnish an explanation of her affective conduct without any reference whatsoever to incest, even of an unconscious sort. Because she was the most stable and the most "understanding" among her brothers and sisters, her mother had associated her with herself in all her cares and responsibilities at a very young age. Laura reached the point where she considered herself so indispensable to the other members of the family that she did not dare be herself any more. She had an unexpressed desire, nevertheless, to break out of her narrow circle of family ties in order to "live her own life." Her friendships were based on this desire. Certain of her friendships symbolized a real revolt against the tyranny of the family. She selected them, as a matter of fact, in strong opposition to the standards in vogue at home. Her *superego*, however, would quickly remind her of her "obligations." Her awkward attempts to get her friends engaged to her brothers only served to manifest her desire to reconcile her dutiful-love for her family with the need she more and more imperiously felt for an affective life that was truly her own.

Between the ages of fifteen and twenty-two, Frances had had three friends. She found it "curious" that she formed close ties exclusively with persons who were nearer her mother's age than they were her own. The psychologist, however, sees nothing curious in this fact. Frances's mother was a woman of intellect, who was very little given to emotional effusions. From all the evidence, it appears that Frances was in need of maternal affection, and that was what older friends could give her.

It can happen that a true friendship may exist between two brothers, between two sisters, or between a brother and a sister. Let there be no mistake about it, however, they are not friends because they have been born of the same parents and have been brought up together. It is actually in spite of all this that they have become friends. For such a friendship to succeed in breaking out of the narcissism of the family circle—which, it seems to me, is the very criterion of any true friendship—the circumstances have to be particularly favorable. It will not succeed unless at least one of the two has already achieved his own liberation, thanks to friendships outside the family. He then can help the other to become extroverted.

Instead of being astonished at the fact that their children "prefer strangers to their own brothers and sisters," intelligent parents are happy about it and do all that they can to encourage it. The principal existential function of friendship is, as a matter of fact, to act as the mediator of affective relations with the outside world.

3. The Bases of Friendship

Like erotic love, and even more so, friendship is born of mysterious affinities which frequently only the unconscious understands. Why did Jonathan, the son of King Saul, experience such an ardent feeling of friendship for David, whose actions were calculated to deprive him of the heritage of the throne of Israel? Why—the fact stands out so clearly in the Gospel—were Lazarus and his sisters, as well as the apostle John, the close friends of Jesus? Let us reflect on our own friendships. Why have such solid bonds of friendship been established between ourselves and certain persons whom frequently we know less well than we know others whom we esteem and admire, but for whom we do not experience any feeling of friendship?

There is no doubt about the fact that David, Lazarus and his sisters, and the apostle John possessed qualities which Jonathan and Jesus respectively appreciated. Our own friends likewise possess intellectual, esthetic or moral qualities which we admire and with which we ourselves are perhaps endowed. There is no reason to suppose, however, that John was valued objectively in the eyes of Jesus more than the other apostles, or that the generosity and piety of the family at Bethany was superior to that of the other families who received the Master at their table. As for our own friends, we know very well that those who are the most dear to us are not necessarily the ones who excel the most in the domains which have the greatest value in our eyes.

Without being hostile to rational clarification by nature, like every other reality of an affective kind, friendship generally eludes its grasp. There must be, in the unconscious of human beings, mysterious affinities which cause two individuals to recognize each other and become friends. There are instances of friendship-at-first-sight which, in appearance, seem hardly different from cases of love at first sight.

The orthodox psychoanalyst refuses to admit that there could be anything in the affective order which eludes his own categories. He finds no difficulty in discovering in each one of our friends either a resemblance or a contrast to one or the other of our parents. He will then have recourse to his favorite explanation, the Oedipus complex, to explain all friendship on the basis of a more or less well disguised expression of incest. We should distrust schemata that oversimplify, however. Their abuse finally ends in explaining nothing. So many people resemble my father or my mother—or are different from them—that I am forced to ask the question, "Why is it precisely this person or that person who has become my friend?"

It seems to me only fair to recognize that no theory can possibly explain any and all cases of friendship. Like every other reality, friendship has its more or less hidden motivations. They have to be sought in the separate unconscious of each individual. And they are never the same for two friendships of even one and the same person.

4. Comparison between Friendship and Love

A comparison between friendship and love is in order. Friendship plays as important a role as love in the affective development of the human person. There are very great similarities, but also very great differences between the two, however, and a comparison will enable us to grasp in a better way the specific nature of each.

As far as can be ascertained with certainty, in the

majority of cases, love does not begin to play its role as a promoter of existence until the age of puberty—that is, at the age when the physical and psychological maturity of individuals has attained a relatively high level. Friendship, on the other hand, very frequently blossoms even at the kindergarten level. It therefore assumes the task of the principal promoter of affective maturation during a particularly delicate phase of life. It is thus influential in preparing the paths which the affective life of the adult will almost inevitably follow.

Parents are very wrong to place obstacles in the path of their children's life of friendship, no matter how well founded their fear may be of their meeting up with evil companions. The risks in this connection are less serious than the ones which are run with regard to the failure of a child to achieve an affective emancipation from his family.

Every psychotherapist knows that among the neurotics of his clientele there is a considerable percentage who were deprived of the pleasures of friendships in their childhood. It is true that it is not always the absence of friendship that causes neurosis; the contrary is just as frequent an occurrence. I mean that it is the neurotic turning in on one's self and a too strong attachment to one's parents (which is equally neurotic in origin) that renders friendship impossible. One of the reasons the psychologist always opposes educating the child at home is precisely the practical impossibility which results from this of the child being able to choose freely his own friends. In such a situation, fixation at the narcissistic stage of emotional development is practically inevitable. This fact deserves to be emphasized all the more because it is usually mothers who are themselves neurotically attached to their child who believe it their duty to spare them the unpleasant aspects of life at school by personally taking charge of their education themselves.

No matter how profound a spiritual communion exists between a man and a woman who are truly in love, it is in the very nature of things that sexual passion will play a very important if not the primary role. As a result, trouble of a more or less serious character is experienced in the region of the higher psychic powers. A lover succeeds in being able to view the one he loves objectively only with great difficulty. M. E. suffered the pangs of jealousy because he was afraid that every man was bent on taking his beloved wife away from him. It seemed inconceivable to him that any man could look at his wife and not desire her. His surprise was great indeed when a man in whom he had profound confidence told him that his wife was completely ordinary and that there was nothing about her that would cause any man to look at her or desire her.

Sex plays little or no role in friendship. Friendship, therefore, is much more lucid and serene than love. A friend is accepted for what he is, with all his defects as well as his good qualities. It is true that we are frequently more indulgent toward the faults of our friends than toward those of individuals to whom we are either indifferent or antipathetic. This is in no way due to any beclouding of our intelligence. It is simply that the affection which we feel for our friends makes it easy for us to understand the reasons for their behavior. Something which is objectively blameworthy can often be excused by someone who knows what the situation is subjectively. In this respect, the benefits of friendship are not limited exclusively to the relationship between friends. A man who experiences a genuine friendship, and who thus penetrates into the subjectivity of another, usually derives from it the benefit of being better able to understand all human beings. He will refuse to judge another "objectively," on the basis of appearances. Indeed, he will make an effort to understand the hidden motives behind his actions. His judgment will be more understanding, because it will feel the effects of the warmth of affectivity. This is the whole secret of the gift of sympathy with which certain individuals seem to have been endowed.

5. Each One Can Have Several Friends

Erotic love establishes a direct bond between two persons. They give themselves to each other totally. It is difficult therefore for the majority of men, and psychologically impossible for most women, to love several persons simultaneously. Polygamy and polyandry are conceivable only within human groups in which sexual possession is not yet intrinsically linked to love. There was no need for a law to require the civilized Moslems of North Africa,

Egypt and elsewhere to renounce polygamy. It passed away of its own accord as soon as their psychological maturity had attained to a sufficiently high level for them to look not only for the pleasure of the senses from a woman but also, and primarily, for spiritual communion with her.

With respect to friendship, the situation is different. As essential as hidden unconscious affinities are for giving birth to it, friendship does not constitute a direct relationship without any intermediary link. If it is a genuine friendship, it presupposes the sharing together of friends in one and the same transcendent reality, in something which surpasses themselves and their friendship. Friends possess the same political or religious ideal, they love the same poets or the same composers. In short, they meet each other on a plane which is extrinsic and superior to themselves.

It sometimes happens that friends are in perfect accord on all the subjects which interest them. That is fine; but perhaps it is not always desirable. Such a friendship runs the risk of losing its dialectical character, and its character of being a means of mutual enrichment. Moreover, in the majority of cases, a friend is the reflection of only one or several of the multiple aspects of one's own personality. This not only makes it possible, but likewise renders it necessary, for each one to have several friends. I experience a communion in depth with my friend X. in relation to our mutual love of music. The fact that he prefers Wagner and I prefer Mozart constitutes no difficulty. Quite the contrary. We are both in a position to understand our respective preferences, and our friendship finds a large part of its nourishment in our mutual exchanges. I also love philosophy, however, while X. does not understand it at all and has no interest whatsoever in it. But this important difference between us does not spoil our friendship. Our friendship finds sufficient nourishment in our mutual love of music. It is from another friendship, with Z., that I derive the necessary stimulation for my philosophical inquiry and reflection. X., in turn, has many other friendships which give him the opportunity to have other kinds of relationships and conversations. And each of my friendships contributes toward the enrichment of all the others.

The richer and more complex a person is, the more

"open" he is in the Bergsonian sense of the term, the more capable he is of enjoying many friendships simultaneously. Men like Emmanuel Mounier, Père Maydieu and Jacques Maritain have enjoyed innumerable friendships simultaneously. Contrary to what the skeptics may say about it, when they said that Mr. X. and Mrs. Z. were their friends, it was not being said in the vague sense in which the term is used in common speech. For them it was a question of real *friends,* that is, men and women with whom they communicated on an existential plane.

Frequently, in the case of those rich individuals who have a gift for friendship, there does not even exist a hierarchy among their different friends. They communicate with each one "in depth," but on a different plane in each case. It may happen that their friends are also friends of one another, and this can result in the existence of a real community of friends. This must not be confused, however, with a group of "chums" or a circle of companions. It is essential, and demanded by the very nature of friendship, that a personal affective communication be established, two by two, among all the members of a community of friendship.

At its height, friendship can become universal. When the Christian declares that Jesus Christ is the intimate and most personal friend of each and every man, he does not mean this in a purely metaphorical sense. One of the most sublime imitators of Christ, Francis of Assisi, seems to have succeeded in establishing a genuine communication of friendship even with the animals and the vegetables, and with the whole of creation.

6. Jealous Friendships

There ought not to be any jealousy present in friendship. What I give of myself to one of my friends does not deprive the others of anything. The absence of jealousy would seem to be a sure criterion of the genuineness of a friendship.

This opinion obviously cannot be shared by those who look upon all friendship as a forbidden erotic attraction in disguise, especially an attraction of a homosexual nature. In reality, the only men and women who are capable of real friendship are those who are clearly heterosexual. If heterosexuality is not clearly present in one of the friends or in both of them, the friendship will never succeed in becoming a profound existential communion, or a very efficacious source of personal enrichment. Such friends naturally experience the torments of jealousy. Instead of looking together toward something transcendent, they mistake each other for the transcendent object. This can only result in disappointment and, sooner or later, in the breaking up of the friendship.

Adolescent friendships frequently are exclusive, and therefore jealous in their character. The reason for this is that they are rarely established on the basis of an ideal or on profound common interests. Adolescents have not yet fully developed their ideals and tastes. It can happen, however, that the two friends will discover together both their ideal and their esthetic tastes. In that case it can be assumed that the unconscious of each of them had mutually recognized the other as being capable of being enthusiastic about the same values.

In spite of its exclusiveness and jealousy, however, adolescent friendship is rarely a disguise for homosexual eroticism. What is true is that among adolescents—and precisely because they are adolescents—such a friendship is susceptible to homosexual deviation, especially in the case of subjects with marked narcissistic traits. But this danger should not be exaggerated.

Two friends of fourteen or fifteen years of age can frequently be observed walking affectionately arm in arm. They write impassioned letters to each other and exchange "confidences." Only an exaggerated desire to systematize everything on the basis of a single principle would take them for unconscious lesbians. There is no question of a true friendship among such adolescents. Usually there does not exist between them any common ideal or profound mutual interest in anything. They have nothing in common, in fact, except their common longing for love. The tender words—and sometimes even caresses—which they shower on the friend are actually directed unconsciously toward the one they are longing for, and whose face they do not as yet recognize. The two young friends display their jealousy and will not tolerate their friend's having other friends. This undoubtedly is less a case of friendship in the true sense of the word than a case of eroticism that is trying to find its way. As a general rule, this sort of friendship, tinged with eroticism, vanishes as soon as one of the two girls falls in love with a man, and all the more quickly if she realizes that she is loved in return by the man in question.

Andrée and Jackie had become "bosom friends" in high school. Jackie was intensely interested in intellectual matters, but she was noticeably retarded on the plane of feminine emotional development. She was seventeen before she experienced her first period and when she was over twenty she still displayed the timidity of a little girl in her relationships with men. Andrée was poor and dressed shabbily. Men hardly noticed her. She thought she was homely and that no man could love her. As college students, the two friends lived together in the same room and could not bear the thought of being separated from each other. On certain days, a great feeling of mutual affection would come over them. Their kisses and caresses, however, never became sexual in character. During vacations they wrote letters to each other almost daily. Their exchanges had nothing superficial about them, moreover, since their interests had had time to develop together. One day, Andrée announced to her friend that a certain young man of their acquaintance had declared his love for her and that she realized that she was in love with him. She protested explicitly that nothing, "absolutely nothing," could be changed in her feelings for Jackie. Jackie, pretending she was not "so ridiculous as to be jealous," nevertheless felt that their friendship could no longer be the same as it had been in the past. This realization, plus a little irritation because Cinedrella-Andrée had met her love before she had, stimulated Jackie to overcome her excessive reserve with regard to men. After the next vacation, she was able to announce to Andrée that she too was in love and was loved in return. The two young women remained friends, because the affinities between them were many and deep. But it definitely put an end to the jealous and exclusive character of their friendship.

Not all adolescent friendships end so happily. Sometimes, as soon as one or both of the friends achieve a heterosexual love relationship, the friends no longer have anything more to say to each other. At other times, especially in the case of women, there can be real scenes when one of them has met the man she loves while the other remains arrested at the infantile stage of an indeterminate love.

7. *Friendship between Men and Women*

Friendship generally exists between persons of the same sex. Some people even believe that there cannot be any true friendship except between men. These generally are women themselves, who judge other women too frivolous and selfish to be capable of entertaining a communion in depth which would exclude all possession not only of what the other person has, but especially of what the other person is. Simone de Beauvoir writes, "Women are comrades in captivity with regard to each other. They help each other to put up with their prison, or even to escape from it. But the liberator will come from the masculine world."[1] There is no friendship between them, just complicity.

On the basis of my own observation, I think that intellectual women are too severe in their judgment about the mass of their sisters, whose "silliness" they exaggerate. There is such a thing as true friendship between women although, as a general rule, it manifests itself in a noticeably different way from the way friendship between men manifests itself. While in masculine friendship, at least among adults, the intellectual or ideological element predominates, in feminine friendships communication usually takes place on the esthetic plane, in the realms of music, literature, or the plastic arts.

Friendship between two persons of the opposite sex presents more of a problem. The majority of moralists and even certain psychologists believe they are suspect, and some of them maintain that such a friendship is radically impossible. This is not my own conviction. Quite the contrary. Whatever the unquestionable difficulties attendant upon it, friendship between a man and a woman frequently is existentially very fruitful. Numerous famous pairs of friends have furnished proof of this fact: Clare and Francis of Assisi, Teresa of Avila and John of the Cross, Jeanne de Chantal and Francis de Sales—and many others, not all of whom were saints.

[1] *The Second Sex*, cf. p. 658 ff.

More so than friends of the same sex, friends of the opposite sex have need of devoting themselves in common to the service of a transcendent ideal and of being enthused about the same values. Otherwise their friendship will infallibly end in failure. The richness of such a friendship depends precisely upon the complementary contribution of each of them to their communion in friendship in a spiritual, intellectual and sensible way.

Since we have just mentioned the sensible element as playing its part in the communion of friendship between a man and a woman, it is clear that the body is not something which is wholly absent in such a friendship. Erotic love itself stands a better chance of succeeding and of lasting longer if it tends to become genuine friendship. As we mentioned before, when we were speaking about conjugal love and the death of love, sexual attraction lasts longer when the partners also communicate with each other on the spiritual level. When, finally, erotic love will nevertheless have ceased to exist, the bonds of friendship between the partners will save them from the painful feeling of failure and emotional frustration.

In the case of the spiritual friendships we have mentioned, the sexual in the proper sense of the term obviously has played no part. Nothing prevents us from admitting, however, that in the unconscious of these saintly friends Eros has had some role to play. We shall have occasion to see in the following chapter how moving mystical love has been in certain instances. Spiritual sublimation has effected such a perfectly successful transformation of Eros in these cases, however, that neither the individuals concerned nor their unprejudiced observers (whether contemporaries or people of a later date) have detected even the slightest direct sign of it.

I personally know of a number of friendships between men and women who are not by any means great mystics or perhaps not mystics at all in any sense of the word. Yet frequently they have succeeded in experiencing a very genuine existential communion in which Eros plays perhaps the same discreet role it plays in the friendship of the saints, but where the sexual in the strict sense of the word has been completely banished. It is also true, however, that frequently enough men and women more or less consciously delude themselves about the "purity" of their friendship.

Mr. Z., a professor, spoke to me with enthusiasm about his wonderful friendship with one of his students. He was married and a sincere, practicing Catholic. He naturally would not permit himself to love the young girl even in a platonic way. He was even persuaded that he did not experience any physical attraction for her. Their friendship was simply a sublime spiritual communion. I was not surprised, however, when several weeks later Mr. Z. told me with great humility and repentance that he and his friend "in some inexplicable way" had become lovers. Such a result is practically inevitable any time that a man and a woman who are friends attempt to prescind from the sexual condition of their natures. Sublimation of the sexual is undoubtedly possible, but it cannot be accomplished either by repression or through ignorance, whether the latter be wilful or not.

The benefits to be derived from friendships between men and women are sufficiently great to prevent one from recommending a timid renunciation of them right from the very beginning. In order that individuals who have attained a certain spiritual level may have a serious opportunity to overcome the dangers which habitually threaten this kind of friendship, it will be enough for them to possess the completest possible lucidity and good faith.

When a woman and a man perceive the dawn of a friendship between themselves, they should know in advance that normally spiritual intimacy will sooner or later lead them to desire physical intimacy as well. The only exceptions to this rule that I have encountered have been in those instances where an appreciable difference of age exists between the two—as is sometimes the case in a friendship between an older master and his young disciple. In the other cases, if the two friends have valid motives of either an objective or a subjective nature for forbidding themselves in a definitive and radical way any sexual love, it should not necessarily be concluded that it is imperative for them to renounce their friendship. Friendship can bring a precious enrichment to their existence. Its realization is possible on condition that they are conscious of the necessity of sublimating the physical.

They must sincerely desire this sublimation and have strength enough to undertake it.

It follows that a "pure" friendship between persons of different sex is undoubtedly feasible, but only between men and women who belong to what has to be called the élite, among whom the so-called higher values are clearly primary. In addition to that, they must have attained to a great enough degree of affective maturity and to an experiential knowledge of themselves.

With regard to young people of the two sexes, there can be no question of a friendship between them, that is, a friendship from which Eros would be banished, unless they agree to live not two by two, but in a group. As I mentioned earlier, there can actually be communities of friends, which are something very different from just bands of chums.

CHAPTER TWELVE

THE SUBLIMATION OF LOVE

MAN'S EMOTIONAL drives are not directed exclusively toward an "erotic object." They are not necessarily directed toward another human person at all, as they are, for example, in the case of friendship. Frequently art, ideas, an ideal, science, one's country, humanity, or God constitutes the object of our love. These can be loved just as much (and at the same time) as a wife or a friend. Certain men actually love one or another of these "higher values" even more than they love a wife, a friend or their own life. There are countless numbers of persons who would gladly give their lives for their country. Others sacrifice an entire life to science or to art, and the list of those who have been martyrs for their religion is a very long one. Psychoanalysis calls such forms of preferential (if not exclusive) love for realities of a sublime character *sublimated love.*

1. The Process of Sublimation

In Freudianism, sublimation is evidently a mechanical process. Various tabus, imposed upon the unconscious by society, prevent certain individuals from directly giving in to the urgings of their instincts. As a result, their psychic energy, or *libido,* makes a detour from its original path and places itself at the disposal of other functions. The popularizers of Freudian doctrine—and there are some excellent practitioners of psychoanalysis among them—have written and spoken more ineptly about the subject of sublimation than about almost any other subject. Affective energy is understood dogmatically to be sexual in its essence. Whereupon ridiculous attempts are then made to explain the works of a Leonardo da Vinci, a Goethe, a St. John of the Cross—and even the Gospel of

211

Jesus Christ—in terms of the presumed sexual conflicts of their authors, such conflicts being frequently manufactured (without the slightest basis in fact) for the sole purpose of substantiating a theory. Is it any wonder then, that under these circumstances many persons of sound judgment, who are not narrow-minded in any way, mistrust psychoanalysis and with it all psychological interpretations of the higher activity of the spirit?

For certain Freudians, the only difference between neuroses and aborted acts on the one hand, and the higher psychic activities on the other, is the fact that the first are inferior and the second are superior to their cause, namely, sexual *libido*. Actually, this is still only a way of speaking, because consistent Freudianism (like materialism and naturalism) is in principle a stranger to any value judgment. The devotion of a Sister of Charity to the poor would "in reality" be no different qualitatively from the panic of a neurotic. Certain psychoanalysts are not afraid to take the leap. They no longer speak of the higher psychic activities in terms of sublimation, but simply in terms of the sexual instinct in disguise.

Divorced from the orthodoxy of pansexualism, the notion of sublimation seems to me to have great psychological value. Consistent with the general conception of *libido* adopted in this book, sublimation would not represent a deviation of sexual *libido* in the direction of taking on the form of a higher activity, but instead an afflux of undifferentiated affective energy carried to the higher functions of the soul. Such an afflux would be as "normal" as the one which carries the *libido* in the direction of sexuality.

The capacity for sublimation is distributed very unevenly among men. It depends strictly upon the degree of talent or genius of the individual. Up to the present time, scientific research has not been able to provide us with a satisfactory explanation of the origin of genius. It is permissible for the man of faith to believe that, in addition to talent and genius, the grace of God can act to direct affective energy toward the heights, putting it at the disposal, for example, of mystical experience.

As everyone knows, there have been mystics and aspirants to mysticism in every religion who have practiced perfect chastity. It would be in vain to try to discover in this fact a confirmation of the Freudian theory of the sublimation of sexual *libido*. Quite the reverse is true. The higher forms of psychic activity are made possible only on the condition that the maximum degree of affective energy is mobilized in their service. Affective energy has to be channeled away from certain—if not all—of its customary outlets. Since eroticism is a great consumer of affective energy, it is inevitable that more will be drawn from this source than from anything else.

It is important to realize that, with the possible exception of certain great mystics, no individual is really in a position to sublimate all of the affective energy that is normally burned up in sexual activity. The depth psychologist hesitates to endorse unreservedly the radical renunciation of sexuality by anyone who is not in the category of the great mystics. I know from experience how serious the danger of neurotic distortion is in the case of those who are not genuinely called to the mystical life, or of those who fail to do all in their power to measure up to the harsh demands which such a vocation can make upon them. Such persons usually are astonished by the strength of their erotic impulses. The bizarre behavior of a great many "old bachelors" and "old maids"—and there are a number of priests and sisters among them—is not unrelated to the fact of their chastity, a chastity that is not counterbalanced by a genuinely mystical life. As Pascal wrote, "He who would play the angel, ends by playing the beast." There is no question of condemning chastity in the name of psychological health. It is simply a matter of pointing out, on the basis of experience, the fact that in normally constituted human beings the *libido* cannot be channeled in a different direction without injury to sexuality unless it finds itself entirely consumed in the service of higher psychic activity.

No one should entertain any illusion about the facility with which such mystical sublimation can be effected. The terrible sexual temptations experienced by St. Anthony in the desert, as well as the temptations experienced by so many other genuine mystics, bear witness to the fact that the saints themselves have not always succeeded without difficulty in consuming all of their *libido* in the flames of divine love. Without casting any doubt upon the genuineness of their sanctity, I must say that there were some saints who were not altogether free from neurotic deviations of their *libido*.

2. The Erotic Symbolism of Mystical Love

Anyone who reads the Bible for the first time (without previous warning) will be surprised to find the Canticle of Canticles among its books. Religion in general—and Christianity in particular—has been represented as standing irrevocably opposed to sexuality. It merely tolerates it because God has seen fit to cause the transmission of life to take place in this way for reasons incomprehensible and scandalous to the human mind. However, here is one of the sacred books in which Eros is actually being glorified!

Without indicating my source, I once recited the following verses to a group of pious Catholics:

> "A kiss from his lips! Wine cannot ravish the senses like that embrace . . .
> To his own bower the king has brought me; he is our pride and boast.
> "Eyes soft as dove's eyes, half-seen behind thy veil; . . .
> Thy lips a line of scarlet, guardians of that sweet utterance; . . .
> Graceful thy breasts as two fawns that feed among the lilies. . . .
> "His left hand pillows my head; his right hand even now, ready to embrace me!
> "Yes, love is a fire no waters avail to quench, no floods to drown. . . ."
>
> (Knox translation)

I read from a recent official Catholic translation (the French translation by Crampon) in which the more obviously erotic expressions had been toned down. The reaction of my listening audience was one of embarrassed silence. They suspected I had read something from Baudelaire or Verlaine, or perhaps from some "immoral" contemporary poet. When I told them it was from the Bible, they hesitated to believe me.

The discussions among exegetes are of little interest to us in the present connection. Some of them maintain that the Canticle is a song of profane love that was inserted into the Bible by singular chance. Others claim that the love which is described in such sensual terms actually refers to mystical love between God and the soul. What interests the psychologist is the fact that first the Synagogue and then the Christian Church retained it as one of the divinely inspired books. It is also remarkable how the greatest of the mystics have all written commentaries on it, filled with infinite devotion. They found in it the perfect expression of their own feelings toward God. How far removed all this is from the prudishness which so frequently tries to impose itself upon men and women in the name of Christian morality!

The metaphors which so many of the well-known Christian and non-Christian mystics have employed to describe the bond that united them to God are, like those of the Canticle, all drawn from the vocabulary of erotic love.

In the sixth century, Saint John Climacus exclaimed, "You have wounded my heart, O love, and my heart cannot bear to suffer your flames."

Saint Angela of Foligno, contemplating an image representing Christ clasping Saint Francis to his bosom, heard Jesus say to her, "This is how I shall clasp you, and much more than one can see with the eyes of the body . . . I shall never leave you if you love me." In another communication, Jesus said to her, "My sweet daughter, my daughter, my beloved, my temple . . . love me, for I love you much, much more than you are able to love me . . . My daughter, my spouse, you are sweet to me. I love you very much."

Madame Guyon, whose influence was great not only on Fénelon, but on the entire religious history of that period in France during which she lived, spoke of her mystical ecstasies in these terms: "Love gave me no rest, not even for a single instant. I said, 'O my love, it is enough, leave me . . .' I desire the love which sends ineffable shudders through the soul, the love which sends me into a swoon . . . O my God, if you would make the most sensual of women feel what I feel, they would quickly forsake their false pleasures for the enjoyment of so true a good."

It will be said that Madame Guyon was an eccentric. She was suspected of being one by Bossuet and other sensible people of her time. Saint Angela of Foligno was hardly a more balanced personality. There is one mystic, however, whose psychological balance is recognized as being superior by Catholic and non-Catholic biographers alike, and that is Saint Teresa of Avila. It is not necessary to have a familiarity with psychoanalysis to comprehend the erotic character of the images Saint Teresa employs in this description of one of her visions:

"The angel held a long golden arrow in his hands. From time to time, he plunged it into my heart and pushed it right down to my entrails. When he withdrew the arrow, it was as if he was going to tear out my entrails with it, and I remained completely on fire with divine love. What I am certain of is that the pain penetrated right down to the very depths of the entrails, and it seems to me that they were torn asunder when my spiritual bridegroom drew away the flesh through which they had been pierced."

Men are usually more sober in giving expression to their mystical states. John of the Cross, however, for all his Spanish chastity and austerity, has recourse to images and symbols which are obviously erotic in inspiration, to describe the sublime beauty of spiritual love:

> Quench thou my griefs. Since none suffices to remove them,
> And let mine eyes behold thee, Since thou art their light and for thee alone I wish to have them. . . .

The Bride:

> My beloved, the mountains. The solitary, wooded valleys,
> The strange islands, the sonorous rivers, The whisper of the amorous breezes.
> The tranquil night. At the time of the rising of the dawn,
> The silent music, the sounding solitude, The supper that recreates and enkindles love.
> Our flowery bed, Encompassed with dens of lions,
> Hung with a purple and builded in peace, Crowned with a thousand shields of gold. . . .
> Beneath the apple-tree. There wert thou betrothed to me;
> There did I give thee my hand. . . .
> And then shall we go forth To the lofty caverns of the rock which are well hidden,
> And there shall we enter And taste the new wine of the pomegranates.

The Spiritual Canticle (E. Allison Peers' translation).

What woman in love would not be happy to receive such verses from her lover? Individuals who never have known any religious experiences can be excused if they conclude from such effusions that mystical love is merely sublimated eroticism. All the more so when it is recalled that the lyrical effusions addressed to God by hysterics are actually nothing more than an unconscious disguise for desires of a specifically sexual nature. Only a depth psychologist who is familiar with religious matters is in a position to distinguish without any difficulty between true and false mystics. (Professor Lhermitte has written a very beautiful and useful work on this subject.) Just because the lucubrations of hysterics clearly proceed from repressed sexual *libido,* there is no reason at all for us to conclude that Teresa of Avila, Angela of Foligno, Henry Suso and John of the Cross were similarly projecting their frustrated sexual desires toward God and the Blessed Virgin.

Detractors of sexuality frequently are individuals who are unconsciously frustrated with respect to erotic love. They show themselves to be just as incapable as the pansexualists of understanding mystical love.

Mrs. H. professed and tried to practice a religion of "pure duty." She mistrusted what she called "pious sentimentality," and found the Canticle of Canticles and similar works obscene. The paintings of the Renaissance depicting the Virgin with her breast uncovered seemed indecent to her. She was scandalized to find them in a number of churches. The very use of the word "love" to describe the relations of the soul with God, or with Christ, was repugnant to her. It made her think of "dirty things." Forgetful of the Canticle of Canticles and of the many images borrowed from the language of eroticism by the prophets, she stated her preference for the Old Testament which, according to her, teaches exclusively the fear of a terrible and far-off God to whom a person would not dare to speak in terms of "swinish things," and with regard to whom the individual has only strict moral and ritual obligations. To her, Christianity—and especially Catholicism—seemed too sensual, and consequently too pagan.

It was not necessary to psychoanalyze Mrs. H. to be

able to detect that she was in the throes of a serious emotional conflict. She was brought up in a very pious, puritanical, Protestant family. When she was a little girl, she had engaged in erotic play with her cousins and one of her brothers. She masturbated intensely during adolescence. As a young girl, she dreamed of love and marriage —a marriage of love. She had the misfortune, however, of encountering men who only wanted to amuse themselves with her. She became pregnant and finally married the last of her lovers. He was not really in love with her, and she was very unhappy with him. As a result of all this, a total confusion of love with what is sordid and forbidden was lodged in her psyche. Tormented by guilt feelings, she looked upon her marital unhappiness as a punishment for her past sins. Was it not on account of the "filthy thing" they call love that she betrayed her parents and all the fine principles they had tried so hard to inculcate in her? Remaining away from the practice of any religion for fifteen years because she considered herself unworthy, she finally sought consolation and a means of expiation in joining a strict religious sect of American origin. In this sect, love was never mentioned. Religion was all a matter of fear and duty!

Mrs. H. discovered neither joy nor peace in this sort of religious life. The more she indulged in austerities, the more she was tormented by her feelings of guilt. She was a sick woman, a victim of a serious neurotic conflict with her *superego*. It was possible for her to be cured, but only on condition that she establish an effective contact with God. She would have to be made to feel that she was in the presence of a God who loves her as his creature and who is completely disposed to forgive her faults. Where, however, would Mrs. H. find the psychic energy she needed to be able to live in a religion of love? She had repressed her sexual *libido*. All of her energy was being blocked by her neurosis. In order for Mrs. H. to love God and to love her fellow human beings in God, it first would be necessary to eliminate her neurotic repression. The *libido* would first have to recover its freedom of movement before it could be given the chance of being orientated in a mystical direction.

3. *Love Sublime*

All who have experienced genuine mystical love are in agreement with St. Paul when he declares that the profound realities of divine love are "ineffable." The categories of human language are erected on the basis of sense experience. We do not find certain things beautiful because we possess the eternal idea of beauty, as Plato thought. It is the other way around. Men find the sight of certain things pleasant, and gradually they come to form for themselves an idea of the beautiful, and finally the idea of absolute beauty. It is permissible to speak of this psychological process in terms of sublimation, provided there is no intended reference to the theories of Freud.

In order to express the ineffable and to translate into human language the affective relation which certain men and women have succeeded in establishing with the Absolute, that is, with God, human beings are forced to have recourse to a terminology and an imagery that is borrowed from sense experience. There are numerous texts in the Bible, in the sacred books of various religions, and in the writings of the mystics in all religions, in which God is described as a magnanimous king, a good master, an infinitely loving father, a leader in battle. Religious souls are aware of how inadequate all such images are in comparison with the reality they are intended to convey. More than any other experience on the natural plane the love between man and woman—the most intense of human experience—is the one that spontaneously supplies the mystics with the images they need in order to communicate their ineffable experience of divine love.

It is true that sexual orgasm has nothing in common with mystical ecstasy. Ecstatics, however, like lovers, feel themselves "transported." For as long as the ecstasy or the orgasm lasts, each of them respectively remains unaware of everything that is alien to their passion. It is astonishing to observe how the mystics, the most famous of whom never personally experienced the joys and torments of erotic love, recognize such feelings so well that they are able to draw on them for such expressive symbols. This is a situation which, to my mind, has not received sufficient attention from the specialists. An important point to remember and to realize is that while certain false mystics, who are more or less hysterical, manifest unmistakable evidence of experiencing a sexual orgasm during their "ecstasy," there is never the slightest indication that this is so in the case of Saint John of the Cross, Saint Teresa of Avila, or any other genuine mystic. Their experience is absolutely unique. It is unparalleled by anything of even the most intense character in natural love.

From the psychological point of view, it is nevertheless undeniable that the affective energy which the mystic consumes in the love of God is the same as that which others make use of in erotic love, friendship and scientific or artistic dedication. Depth psychology can give us no knowledge of what is specifically divine in mystical love, but it does enable us to understand and to explain the purely human aspects of it. If there are important differences to be found in the writings of different mystics, both Christian and non-Christian—and there most certainly are such differences—these would seem to be due not so much to God, the other term of the mystical communion, as to the "quantity" and the "quality" of the affective energy of individual mystics. They would be due also to their respectively different human experiences, their education, and the influences of the civilization in which they lived.

Anyone who examines the different manifestations of mystical love without prejudice will have to admit that it is impossible to speak about them in terms of sublimation in the Freudian sense. Even the notion of sublimation which has been adopted in this book has to be employed in this connection with an infinite amount of precaution. In mystical love, the affective powers of man find themselves transported to a level which has nothing in common with even the most remarkable natural capacities. We speak of sublimation of affective energy in reference to realities in one and the same natural order. As we saw before when everything sexual has been excluded, friendship between a man and a woman can be considered an example of an affection that has been sublimated. In the case of mystical love, however, to be very precise, there is really no question of something that is being sublimated, but of something which is in itself *sublime*.

INDEX

abortion, 166, 172
Adler, Alfred, 137
aggression, 132–137
androgynous form, 23–26, 44–48
Angela of Foligno, St., 215, 216, 217
Animality, 28, 32, 54, 64, 119, 189

Balzac, Honoré de, 44
Baudelaire, Pierre Charles, 214
Beauvoir, Simone de, 24, 45, 46, 103, 107, 134, 165, 207
bed, double, 161
Bergson, Henri, 51, 203
Bossuet, Jacques Bénigne, 215
Breton, André, 35
Breuer, Josef, 99
Byron, George Gordon, 44, 171

Canticle of Canticles, 214–215, 217
castration complex, 61, 118
Catherine the Great, 180
Cayrol, Jean, 42
celibacy, 170, 212–213
chain love, 171–184; Don Juan, 171–179, 180, 183; Messalina, 179–184
Chantal, Jane de, 69, 207
Clare, St., 69, 207
Claudel, Paul, 160

courtly love, 32, 140

Dalbiez, Roland, 82, 87, 99
David, King, 199
divorce, 38, 58, 163, 165, 173, 175, 181, 185, 187
Don Juan (archetype), 52, 171–179, 180, 183
Dumas, Alexander, 171

Elizabeth I, 180
Engels, Friedrich, 139, 166
Existentialist theory, 132–135, 138, 189

fathers-in-law, 153–154
Fénelon, François de Salignac, 215
Francis de Sales, St., 69, 207
Francis of Assisi, St., 69, 204, 207, 215
free love, 164–167
Freud, Sigmund, 23, 27–28, 36, 53, 61, 63, 76, 79, 81–82, 84–87, 91–92, 93, 96–97, 99, 137, 141, 180, 189, 193, 219
Freudians, 76, 81, 93, 118, 141, 154, 194, 197–198, 211–212
friendship, 27, 65, 68, 162, 194–210, 211, 220
frigidity, 29, 68, 73, 105, 120, 121n, 126–129, 136, 160, 161, 181–183

frustrations, 112–137; absence of physical pleasure, 125–130; emotional refusal of love, 112–117; fear of love, 117–120; hatred, 132–137; illusion, 120–125, 126, 149, 189, 190; sexual initiation, 128

Garbo, Greta, 64
Goethe, Johann Wolfgang von, 211
Gogol, Nikolai Vasilievich, 106
Goldoni, Carlo, 171
Guyon, Jeanne Marie de la Motte, 215

hatred, 132–137, 187, 191
Hegel, Georg Wilhelm Friedrich, 132
Heidegger, Martin, 134
Henry III, 51
homeliness, 54, 57, 115
homosexuality, 96–100, 101, 105–106, 194, 204–205

illegitimacy, fear of, 144, 160, 172
impotence, 110, 160–161
incest, 76–90, 99, 100, 154, 197–198, 200; between brother and sister, 87–90
independence, 46, 155–157, 168–170
indifference, 188, 191
inferiority complex, 58–60, 179
Islamic countries, customs, 97, 202

Jansenism, 30, 32
Jaspers, Karl, 192
jealousy, 35, 40, 43, 64, 65, 83, 98, 114, 124, 129–131, 154, 179, 195, 201, 204–206
Jesus Christ, 199, 204, 212, 215
John Climacus, St., 215
John of the Cross, St., 69, 207, 211, 216–217
John, St., 199

Jonathan, 199
Jung, Carl Gustav, 23, 25–26, 86, 135, 171, 194

Kierkegaard, Soren, 138, 139
Knox, Ronald A., 214
Kolontai, Alexandra, 166

Laforgue, Réné, 180
La Rochefoucauld, François de, 137
Lazarus, 199
Lenin, Nikolai, 191
Leonardo da Vinci, 180, 211
lesbianism, 54, 57, 100–106
Lévy-Bruhl, Lucien, 141
Lhermitte, Léon Augustin, 217
libido, 27, 55, 92–93, 137, 161–162, 194–196, 211–214, 217, 218
Ligneries, Françoise de, 108
loneliness, 116–117
Louis XIV, 191
love: at first sight, 55–56; biochemical reaction, 26–28, 36; courtly love, 32, 140; death of, 185–193; feminine predisposition, 44–48; first love, 34–38, 41, 54, 55, 62, 64, 66–68, 93, 100; inability to, 39; loss of objectivity, 39–41; mystical, 214; psychological basis, 23–26, 30–34, 105; reciprocity, 41–44; seasonal, 54–55; sexless spiritual communion, 28–31, 32–34, 36, 68–70, 70–72, 161, 190; sublime, 70, 211–220
Lucka, Emile, 32

Maintenon, Françoise d'Aubigné, 191
Malraux, André, 131
Maritain, Jacques, 204
marriage, 138–170; annoyance of daily routine, 157–159; social institution, 139, 164; autonomous wive[s] 168–169; children as deter-

rents, 147–152, 167; choice of mate, 42, 49–62; divorce, 163–165; end of, 163–166; eroticism in, 160–163, 166; free love, 164–167; historical separation from love, 138–142; in-laws, 152–155; modern attitude, 142–147, 155, 168–170; self-realization in, 155–157, 167–170

Marx, Karl, 139
masochism, 106–111, 133
masturbation, 36, 94–95, 218
Mérimée, Prosper, 171
Messalina, 179–184
Molière, 171
Montherlant, Henri de, 138, 171
motherhood, 61, 147–152
mothers-in-law, 152–155
Mounier, Emmanuel, 204
Mozart, Wolfgang Amadeus, 203

narcissism, 92–96, 103–104, 112, 179, 196, 199
Nietzsche, Friedrich Wilhelm, 44

Oedipus complex, 23, 53, 55, 63, 76–90, 99, 200; archetype, 76–77

paraphiliae, 91–111
Pascal, Blaise, 213
Paul, St., 219
Peers, E. Allison, 217
Péguy, Charles Pierre, 142
Plato, 23, 24, 29, 63

platonic love, 37, 63–75; adults, 68–70, 98, 174; children, 63–68, 101; neurotics, 70–75; parental, 78
Plisnier, Charles, 115
polygamy, 202
Ponte, Lorenzo da, 171
prostitution, 66, 116

Rostand, Edmond, 171

sadism, 106–111, 133
Saliège, Cardinal, 31
Sartre, Jean-Paul, 132–134, 136
scorn for the body, 29–31, 32–33, 68, 73–74, 78, 142
Self-realization in marriage, 46, 155–157
Sister of Charity, 212
Stekel, Wilhelm, 121, 135, 183
Stendhal, Henri Beyle, 54
sublimation, 30, 32, 69, 70, 211–220
suicide, 166, 172
superego, 36, 148, 183, 189, 197–198, 218
Suso, Henry, 217

Talleyrand, Charles Maurice de, 180
Teresa of Avila, St., 69, 207, 216, 217
Tirso de Molina, 171

Valéry, Paul Ambroise, 142
Verlaine, Paul, 214
Violet, Abbé, 30

Wagner, Richard, 203

Other MENTOR-OMEGA Books